7 49 10D 25

# VICTORIAN WORCESTER

## A BIOGRAPHY

Jeff Carpenter

First published in 2006 by
Brockhill Publishing
Unit 3C. Shrub Hill Industrial Estate
Worcester, WR4 9EL

ISBN: 0-9552571-0-7

Printed by Now Print - second edition June 2006

A catalogue record of this book is available from the British Library

# Contents

## Biography of Victorian Worcester

# Biography of Victorian Worcester

They did things differently then. In 1895 Greswolde - Williams living out at Broadwas Court felt his tame Indian bear was no longer tame enough. It had started biting and scratching but Greswolde –Williams was unperturbed. Was there not an efficient railway system in this country? His gardener knocked up a packing case and the unfortunate animal was promptly sent off to a zoo from Worcester's Shrub Hill Station.

But today looking back over the scene, you wonder if those who crowd in to enjoy the fun of our Victorian Christmas Fair might appreciate something beyond the token bowler hats and the fancy neckerchiefs and might wish to explore the fascinating story of Worcester's Victorians and what made them 'tick.' Like every city of the time, this was a place in the grip of profound changes and its authorities were often unsure whether to stick to the old or embrace the new. The book investigates some key features of life in the Worcester community: work and leisure, poverty and prosperity, religion, transport and education. There are chapters on building development and drink with an additional section on some of Worcester's own specialities like porcelain, sauce and Elgar.

A work like this for the general reader relies heavily on the labour of others, which I gratefully acknowledge. Hopefully the text will find some favour amongst those who love Worcester. It has been written as a biography rather than a formal local history. Is that cheating or trying to get round the rules of historical rigour? I trust not. The aim was to gain that bit more flexibility -to make the book more readable.

# Links with the Past

Nineteenth-century Worcester was the most traditional of cities. Despite all the bustling new commerce and industry it seemed almost impossible to shake off the past. One famous landmark, finally levelled in 1843, was the old castle mound which for centuries had loomed over the riverbank. But when Queen Victoria came to the throne in 1837, a surprising amount of the city's historic fabric remained standing. It was also a townscape still bursting with greenery and garden plots. The urban suburbs of the future were then only a scatter of satellite rural villages and this atmosphere of semi-rustication characterised whole swathes of the city right up to the end of the century. It explains why Edwin Lees and his merry band of fellow naturalists were able to romp about Worcester, listening with delight to the sound of the nightingale along the banks of Laugherne Brook. They also got absorbed in scraping off squadrilus, an old variety of ragwort from the high riverside walls below the cathedral. It was a plant which Edward Lees believed could have spread there from the potherb garden of the ancient medieval priory itself.

Up to this point the city had remained at a comfortable size. But although the numbers in certain central parishes were now falling, the general population trend was relentlessly upwards as Worcester expanded outwards, swallowing up its surrounding villages. A 'liberty post', standing at the southern corner of Salt Lane (Castle Street), which marked the old boundary line had no further purpose. In 1837 they decided to increase Worcester's urban area by nearly four times, so that Barbourne Brook and the Swan Inn now marked the new city limits to the north. In 1835 the area round the Cathedral was absorbed into the city, having lost its jealously guarded territorial status in the Hundred of Oswaldslaw.

As for the Victorian inhabitants, many owned surnames with true local pedigrees like those ending in 'ard'. And the local speech still reflected the strong cadences of old Mercian Saxon language – 'Hers a right scrat, her is' (a hard working wench). Incomers from the villages were an important element of the expanding population. Like Elgar's sister, Lucy, they would keep their love of the country ways – in her case 'the refreshment and tranquil pleasure' of breathing the air of Broadheath Common.

For many city residents keeping up old rural practices was hardly a problem. The authorities according to the antiquarian, John Noake, just about managed to introduce some control over the many pigs wandering about the streets. How well and truly the citizens knew and loved their porkers. Words long forgotten were then common, like 'trinkley' – a small fat pig and 'mudgin' – the fat off a pig's chitterling. Old custom surrounded pig breeding such as the rule that no animal should be slaughtered when the moon was waning or the bacon would not be nice and plump. As late as 1890 the developer, E F West, was putting in pig sties in Radcliffe Street just as today we would be installing garage spaces. When illnesses came, local people would always be keen to try the old remedies first. Physicians at the Royal Infirmary despaired over the popular devotion to folk medicine like the Worcester cure for shingles which was rubbing on dust and grease from round the clapper of an old church bell. These customs kept things steady in a changing world, and those in power were quite adept in using them. The ancient parish of St Helen's kept up a regular custom of beating the bounds and St Helen's curfew bell was rung nightly – as in medieval times. Its rival was the 'Plum pudding bell' which sang out from the tower of St Martin's in the Cornmarket.

There were many other ancient practices. Destitute widows and spinsters claimed the right 'to go a Thomasin' – the old begging of alms on the Feast of St Thomas just before Christmas. And at Christmas itself there was the merrymaking of 'Lambswool' – letting toasted apples drop down into a heady mixture of spiced ale. In the streets of Dolday just before Easter they celebrated the old cult of Eavin or Heaving where six lasses waylayed some likely lad and tied him to a chair already bedecked with ribbons. After hoisting him in the air and whirling him round several times he would be let down but only released after paying beer money to each of his charming captors. Another example of local folklore was manifested in the account of a wedding reported in *The Worcester Herald* of February 24th, 1844. George Gould, charged at the Petty Sessions with firing off volleys of blank cartridges at the nuptials of a Miss Bright, offered a robust defence. These loud shots, he argued, were part of the 'liberties of the subject'. City authorities liked life to run to an ordered code. The official alternative motto was 'Mutare Sperno' – 'I despise change' and those prepared to accept the old order, however poor, might expect to benefit from Worcester's benevolent citizens who had founded so many historic alms and charities. Aid could come from Berkeleys, Jarvis, Shewringes, Nashs, Walsgraves, Wyatts or from many other funds. There was a special help for young women in peril of prostitution and Hebbs Charity was set up to aid 'decayed councillors and aldermen and their dependents'.

# Old Trades and Old Ways

As in previous centuries goods and services came into town from the surrounding countryside. Thomasons Wharf supplied Highley best coal or tops at 15s 6d a ton as well as local bricks and tiles. The provision of food was a major priority. Worcester people had always enjoyed their eating and traditional dishes were those they fancied most. In the year Victoria came to the throne there were 54 butchers in the town and 17 cheesemongers from whom you could choose something tasty. The local fish delicacy was the lampern or eel caught in wicker putcheons set down deep in the Severn mud. For those with a sweet tooth there were Worcester Fat Cakes – lardy buns which had once been a favourite temptation of the 18th-century actress Sarah Siddons. That anonymous 18th-century cookery book *The Worcester Caterer and Cook* mentions two excellent soups – one a pea soup, and the other a herb soup which took seven and a half hours in preparation and was made with a knuckle of veal, sorrel, endive, onions, sweet herbs, a ham bone, cloves, mace, and asparagus tops.

The food shops were always plentiful yet folk also loved their Worcester markets. The annual Hop and Cheese Fair took place in Angel Square and Angel Street despite the fearful crowds, and St John's still possessed its own Mop or Hiring Fair. There were also special markets like the famous one for hops and the weekly market for cattle which in 1838 was moved off the streets onto a special site. There was also a flower market, and one for 'green stuff' and poultry. This was a spot from which Feargus O'Connor, the Chartist leader, once looked out from his vantage point in a nearby tavern, enjoying the hustle and bustle and fortified by a glass of brandy with two eggs in it.

Worcestershire was renowned for its traditional varieties of fruit and vegetables. That most experimental of 19th-century growers, John Williams, gave us amongst others the Pitmaston Duchess Pear, the Pitmaston Champagne Goosebery, and the Bruce Potato. Richard Smith who became one of Britain's largest seed suppliers was advertising in his 1901 seed catalogue the Worcester Swede as one of his specialities at 1/2d per pound.

Despite the economic advances of the Victorian period, the older trades and callings still lived on. Mrs Henry Wood wrote about the tallow candle makers in her novel, *Mildred Arkell*, and not far from the Cathedral there was the well known fishermen's colony in Frog Lane with the predictable timber yards, boatbuilders, and ropewalks located further along the riverside.

It has been estimated that by the 1880's there were over three million horses in Britain. Many local businesses associated with horses were found off the Butts and up the London Road:- farriers, vets, livery stables, saddlers, and providers of fodder. A kindred activity was the well known horsehair carpet manufactory in Birdport with its horsehair room and die house.

Worcester was also a centre for traditional clothing. In 1837 it possessed nine clog and patten makers and was famed for its military tailoring and outfitting services to the aristocracy and clergy. In 1900 the firm of Whitehead and Sons was still proudly advertising their 'ancient standing – as representatives of the sartorial profession – perfectionists in liveries and in matters of style and finish'.

In matters of administration, the late nineteenth century was a time of considerable change. In 1888 the Lord Salisbury cabinet (without much enthusiasm from Salisbury himself) decided to grasp the nettle of modernising county local government. Many powers which affected everyone's lives were removed from the old quarter session authority and handed over to the County Borough located in the Guildhall and to the Worcestershire County Council at the Shire Hall – an enclave of county territory carved out of the City.

Much of the change was only skin deep, for the influence of the historic landowning families at the Shire Hall was certainly not defunct. It might appear to be an elected council but many of their number were county aldermen who had been selected off an approved list of names drawn up by Earl Beauchamp, Worcestershire's premier peer. Thus when this august body first met, all county council members with landowning pretensions found themselves seated upon a special dais raised above the rest. And every working morning, Martin, the butler employed at the Shire Hall Judge's Lodgings, would descend and gently guide elderly county members up the steps before they began their business of making local democracy work. It would seem that tradition still reigned in Worcester however fast the forces of change might be moving elsewhere.

# Keeping Worcester Happy

## A Survey of Victorian Entertainment

Worcester people loved to enjoy themselves and they wanted their entertainments ever bigger, better, and more sensational. John Noake, the celebrated local historian, commemorated this zest for pleasure by giving over two chapters of his *Worcester in Olden Times* (1849) to a description of the local historic sports, festivities, plays, and pageants. In Victorian times some of the high days and holidays were still celebrated. Most notably the old Hiring Fair over at St Johns and the Hop and Cheese Fair which each September crowded certain inner city streets to bursting point.

Wakes and fairs throughout Worcestershire had always been notoriously exuberant. For instance, wayward young adventurers tempted over to celebrate in Kidderminster would certainly be walking on the wild side. All their games were pursued with extreme vigour, including 'dancing for pumps', climbing greasy poles for legs of mutton, and catching the soaped pig. For the amusement of quieter natures there was grinning through a horse-collar and eating rolls oozing with hot treacle.

## More Fairs and Spectacles

In Worcester the wonders of the fair – galloping horses, swing boats, and shooting galleries, possessed a special magic because this was the winter base for Stricklands' – best known of all regional funfair operators. Their headquarters was lodged in a large rooming house at 20 Newport Street, and their fair equipment was stored under the railway viaduct from whence it was moved and set up with the precision of a military exercise.

Excitement ran equally high when a circus hit town with its long colourful procession, exotic animals, and a variety of freak shows for which our Victorian forebears had a special weakness. Sangster's Circus came in 1890 and one of its enthusiastic patrons was Elgar's brother-in-law, Charles Pipe. Despite his respectable image as a grocer, he was entranced by the wonder of *Chang the Chinese Giant* and *Tom Thumb and his Wife*. He nonetheless confessed in his diary just a few reservations –'some of the circus freaks' he wrote, 'are not at all nice to look upon'. To the pleasure of many citizens there were popular spectacles which came entirely free. In her novel, *Mrs. Halliburton's Troubles*, Mrs Henry Wood gives a graphic description of the hullabaloo which greeted the ceremonial arrival of the judges when their carriages drew up at the Guildhall for the start of the assizes. Another event was Oak Apple Day when the Guildhall gates were festooned with greenery followed by a curious folksy procession. Representatives of almost every trade marched through the streets accompanied by Mayor and Corporation – no doubt an attempt by the authorities to affirm the existence of public unity in difficult times.

A ready audience could always be guaranteed for celebrities. In 1843 the whole town turned out for the Dowager Queen Adelaide when she came to the theatre. To the relief of those in control, there was one who never came. The Italian hero Garibaldi was so wildly popular that two Worcester pubs were named after him, even though he missed the City out during his famous British tour.

# Sport

By the end of Victoria's reign, sporting fixtures were increasingly popular even though the support of influential patrons still counted heavily. In racing the backing of the Croome Estate was a particular boon. Lord Coventry was a passionate enthusiast and the Coventry Stakes for two year olds was always a red letter day in the Pitchcroft racing calendar. The 9th Earl's own racehorses were devotedly trained on the specially constructed gallop at Pirton and frequently sported on the Worcester course in their colours of brown and blue.

Boxing on the other hand never regained the glories of the world championship bout on Pitchcroft in 1824. That bruising, bare-knuckled battle of endurance between Spring and Langan had lasted many hours with the riotous crowd of forty thousand spectators comprising about twice the size of the city's entire population. Casualties from the enormous crush had been rushed to the nearby Royal Infirmary only to find that all available 'medics' were away watching the fight!

Enthusiasm for cricket began quietly enough. An episode from the very early days is delightfully captured in a canvas of 1852 by W L Bowden. In a match against the visiting All England XI, there are no pads, no batting gloves and no marked boundaries; the players are all wearing top hats and the bowling is by means of underhand lobs. The County Cricket Club was formally instituted in 1865 at a meeting in the Star Hotel and was soon blossoming under the shrewd patronage of the wealthy Paul Foley. By 1899 it had gained the status of a first-class county. Although there were now professional players and officials,

Worcestershire was still famed for its talented amateurs. Of particular renown were the Foster brothers. 'Mr R E Foster', explained one commentator, 'possesses almost every quality: strong defence, self restraint free, attractive style and wonderful wrist shots. He has carried pulling to a fine art'. Probably the most critical factor of all was the new permanent ground at New Road where the estimable Fred Hunt as chief groundsman, spent all his hours transforming a former chunk of rough pastureland into an area of sacred sporting turf.

Football too was coming into its own. Most of the small Worcester clubs were associated with a local church or chapel or pub – worthwhile but ephemeral. Two of the larger sides Berwick Rangers and Worcester Rovers decided to amalgamate to form the Worcester City Club. They were wise enough to employ the services of Harry Yoxhall as their first club secretary – very much the new style of capable sporting official. Worcestershire football benefited greatly from the big breweries. They were more than ready to provide sponsorship and the club trophies. To their profit, the brewers realised – sport and beer went naturally together.

For anyone desirous of building up their physical stamina there was the Worcester Gymnastic Club which put on a fine public display in honour of the Queen's Diamond Jubilee celebrations in 1897.

A very prominent new craze was for cycling which had the merit of catering for the ladies too. Some clubs were actually associated with local cycle manufacturers. The Porcelain Works sported a group of seventy-five members in 1894, and the cycling club over at St Johns was as vigorously prestigious as any in the Midlands.

Much enjoyment was to be had from the River Severn. The Ariel Boat Club founded in 1841 was one of the earliest in England. At the time of Worcester's first regatta in 1845, three more were in existence and by 1876 members of the famous Worcester Rowing Club had also taken to the water. On Gala days the river bank was crammed with spectators. Newspaper reports describe 'gaily prankt' barges moored alongside with a medley of canoe and punt races with heavy side betting to add spice.

Swimming in the Severn had always been a rough and tumble affair with children plunging headlong from two rafts located off Pitchcroft. Now a more demanding public taste insisted upon more pampered arrangements including a proper swimming pool combined with facilities for hot baths and massage. The result was a profitable business venture initiated by a complete newcomer, Mr Barber of Cheltenham, because earlier in the 19th century Cheltenham had emerged as a premier spa resort where the local newspapers proudly blazoned their weekly tally of dukes, duchesses, marquises, earls, counts, and foreign titles in residence. In 1889 Mr Barber was bought out by William Park who further developed this lively business venture by offering an exotic choice of Turkish bath, sulphur iodine pit, calomel and electric treatment, and nature cure.

## 'The Applause, Delight and Wonder of our Stage'

Worcester had always given its warmest approval to the performing arts. If Victorian audiences were harder to please and reputations harder to earn, it was because live entertainment was so close and immediate to everyday life. The centre of activity was still the Theatre Royal plushly rebuilt in 1875 by C J Phipps, one of the top designers in the business, whose improvements created something like the red velvet roominess of a Venetian Palazzo. Immediately before this the theatre experienced leaner times. Henry Bennett, the proprietor, might have been influential on the Corporation but he was notoriously mean, and his productions lacked the calibre and distinction of former Regency days. On one occasion this theatre owner staged the battle scene from Macbeth entirely without props, the fight taking place in a room decked out for the next performance with flowers neatly arranged on a table. The glory of the Theatre Royal came from its visiting companies who arrived by train bringing with them extensive quantities of fascinating scenery. In this way Worcester audiences came to be dazzled by such giants of the thespian arts as Henry Irving, Charles Mathews, J L Toole and the famous Black American tragedian, Morgan Smith. There were also yearly visits by the D'Oyly Carte with their Gilbert and Sullivan and frequent appearances by the great Shakesperian Company owned by Frank Benson.

The mid-1880's brought William Gomershal to town - 'the Sultan of Angel Street' as he became known. Gomersal was an astute actor manager who inspired his audiences with a passion for the popular stage. Laying on bravura performances of everything from Shakespeare to melodrama , he delighted most of all with his pantos. He was even prepared to whip up patriotic fervour if it helped the box office. And so at a dramatic point in the Boer War with feelings running high, we find Gomershal striding onto the stage, dressed as General Lord Roberts and bearing the Union Jack, as he delivered a rousing oration in praise of Britain's imperial war effort.

Edward Elgar's versatile talent prepared him from the outset to search out every opportunity for making music. His work all too soon caused him to move away but his Worcester upbringing left an indelible mark. He might complain against elements of the local musical establishment but was stimulated by his involvement with the Three Choirs. Starting humbly with the 'band' of violins at a festival rehearsal in 1878, he was soon standing in the Cathedral conducting his own composition, *Froissart*. This was followed in 1899 by the successful launch of the *Enigma Variations*, a work replete with references to Worcestershire characters. Elgar was closely integrated into the local musical scene. Residing for some years at 4 Field Terrace, the home of his sister and her husband, he worked at the family music shop, taught his private pupils, and even trained an orchestra out at Powick Asylum. His brother-in-law, Charles Pipe, recounts in his diary the variety of popular music then readily available:– glee clubs at the Crown and the Unicorn and concerts at the Public Hall.

With theatres subjected to severe regulations on anything mildly risky, many performers now turned to the music hall. Vesta Tilley and her glittering music hall career symbolised the new trend. Born in Worcester as Matilda Powles, she was immersed almost immediately into the traditions of show business. Hers was a poor family with thirteen children but her father himself was unusually resourceful and talented. Taking the stage name, Harry Bell, he appeared as a tramp musician accompanied by

Fatso, 'the incredible performing dog'. He was to be her guide in the early years. Vesta Tilley soon left her home town for wider horizons but never lost touch. The strong early influences were those which shaped her working life and to reinforce the Worcester connexion she married Walter de Frece, whose father had owned the Alhambra music hall. 'The Great Little Tilley' was always brilliant in playing to working class audiences and her tear jerker medleys like *Near the Workhouse Door* were executed with faultless timing. Well known for her male impersonations, she squeezed herself into a small gent's evening suit 'no larger than would fit an ordinary rabbit' as she explained. She became famous for mimicking and sending up male audiences, somehow charming her way into the hearts of those who had come to be scandalised. In collaboration with her husband, later Sir Walter de Frece, Vesta Tilley set out to raise the tone of the music hall nationally. They aimed to transform the image particularly that of the low dives or 'penny gaffes'. Audiences found new style notices appearing: 'Please do not use strong language here'. Eventually Tilley became amongst the highest paid artistes in Britain. It was a long way from the poor streets of the Worcester Blockhouse.

# City of Work

Someone looking out over the riverbank in 1900 would have been struck by the sprawl left behind by over a century of industrial development. The Cathedral still presided majestically over the skyline but it was a skyline full of smoke from factory and domestic chimneys.

Work was basic to life and Victorian cities bred jobs by the multitude, despite all the bouts of heavy unemployment. True, everyone wanted a decent wage but the dependability of the work was even more important. For females, especially, the tempting solution was to go into domestic service. Even in harsh times there were usually vacancies about and in Worcester, quite modest households often employed two servants. Those looking for 'a position' would certainly need to be 'recommended' and armed with a reference; they were likely to start their search through the columns of the local newspaper. This advertisement from Berrows Worcester Journal for January 1879 gives us a flavour of what they might find. 'Required: Assistant Housekeeper must be fond of children; good knowledge of cooking and plain sewing and make herself generally useful'. Wage figures from the similar sized cathedral city of Exeter show how in 1871 a 'good plain cook' would be earning £14 a year in addition to her keep. A parlour maid, starting off, would get £7 a year plus her keep but a butler might expect to be offered as much as £61. On occasions there might be extras. Francis Kilvert recalls in his Diary how his Worcester Aunt Maria bequeathed £100 each to two servants but not to the cook – 'a bad tempered woman' who was ignored except for the £5 'for mourning'.

Many other Worcester jobs were heavily dependant on the old historic trades with their traditional craft skills. Often these would be located along the bank of the River Severn like the rope walks and saw mills. A local directory for 1851 also mentions the 74 residents living in Severn Street whose livelihood was still connected to the Severn fishing. Practised in the time-honoured fishing techniques, they tended to operate in teams employing the Severn Long Net – a plain sheet of netting with two men stationed up front – 'the headers' and two men at the back end – 'the muntlers'. Earning a living meant struggling against severe restrictions imposed on fishermen's rights by big landowners. In spite of such difficulties, Severn salmon were freely caught and sold both in shops and on the streets off the backs of fishermens' donkeys at sixpence a pound.

The biggest local employment was gloving, an industry with origins going back to the 13th century when New Street was then known as Glover Street. By the early 19th century, the City was characterised by a number of scattered small firms. But the industry needed to modernise or die because there was such serious competition from elsewhere in Britain and abroad. Almost as problematic were the fickle changes in fashion which made manufacturers uncertain about risking further capital investment. Before 1826 the trade went through a relatively expansive stage but that was followed by years of deep depression. As a result the bigger factories like Dent and Fownes cornered a giant share of the market. By 1885 there were only eleven main producers locally, where a few years previously, there had been a hundred and eighty.

The big firms used more machinery, concentrating most of the core work inside their factories. It was now the skilled male cutter who played the dominant role but he needed to be assisted by the labour of between twelve and fifteen female sewers. Outwork did not disappear because such big manufacturing firms simply could not have coped without their army of gloveresses operating from home. In 1851 the small hamlet of Warndon accommodated thirteen such gloving outworkers, with some 96 living in the village of Crowle. Their handiwork demanded fastidious care and be they parers, pointers, stakers or sewers, they toiled hard, long hours for their small wage packets.

From our modern perspective the gloving industry seems to have encompassed some decidedly odd processes. In the 1880's Dents were still using millions of eggs each year to 'dress' their fine leathers from tough skins which were sometimes even softened up with urine. Fownes who had moved up from London were proud to advertise their extensive range of finished leathers including Paris, glace, kid and pure suede, offering some extremely fancy linings as an additional option. There were numerous varieties from which to select. There were gloves for the military, for formal dances, and dress occasions. Councillors wore them on civic parade, and there were special pairs for tennis and cycling. Fownes and Company, anxious to claim some extra degree of exclusivity, announced that they kept in stock special separate pattern sizes for fitting out each member of the royal household.

The iron industry was not restricted to the Black Country to the north where Worcestershire impinged upon the South Staffordshire Coalfield. Iron was also produced locally, and the night time streets of the Blockhouse glowed with the light of its furnaces. The principal foundry of Hardy and Padmore helped satisfy an almost insatiable demand for objects of cast iron. For domestic consumption there were stoves, firegrates, footscrapers, hearth ornaments, and garden furniture, somewhat unkind to the human posterior. And for business use there were larger stoves, iron stairways – spiral or straight – and even a Hardy and Padmore engine which was never effectively marketed and sold. The firm struck lucky in its sales to newly established municipal councils. These required a wide range of products fabricated from cast iron: street lamps, railings, manhole covers, and iron seats for the park. This firm's most prestigious commission was for the set of iron railings surrounding the Royal Pavilion in Brighton. Worcester possessed two elaborate examples of their castings; firstly the floridly designed fountain inside the market hall and secondly the large ornate clock which hung on the outside.

So much of the City's intense new industrialisation in engineering and railways derived from metal founding. In 1869 at the height of a frantic but short-lived existence, the Worcester Engine Works employed up to one thousand men – including the heavy gangs occupied in producing huge and intricate iron castings. The financial collapse of this promising enterprise focused even more attention on the neighbouring industrial site of Mackenzie and Holland. They were the owners of the Vulcan Works and manufacturers of railway signals together with a whole variety of kindred requirements from oil cans to railway gates and signal boxes. Some of the other local foundries set their sights more humbly, hoping to satisfy the needs of farmers. Brettels and Evans and Larkworthy became specialists in iron agricultural implements and made ploughs and harrows, scuffles, horse shoes as well as robust iron mills for crushing oil cake to feed the cattle.

Worcestershire was also a traditional centre for tin plate and other coated metal products. The Baldwin works were sited to the north of the County but raised their financial capital from Worcester banks. The most significant development was an entirely new arrival in 1855 when William Blizzard Williamson relocated from Wolverhampton bringing all his skilled workmen, technical expertise, and business acumen into the run-down Blockhouse district. By the end of the century Williamson's had gained a lion's share of the dynamic new market in tinned goods. From their Providence Works, the company turned out a wide range of tin plated dairy churns, dairy equipment, and domestic items like tin trunks and baths as well as meeting the public demand for new style tobacco tins.

The early years of Victoria's reign had proved times of opportunity for the industrial chemist. Their largest Worcester venture was the Hill and Evans Vinegar Works squatting across Lowesmore like some large London brewery complete with giant vats, granary and mashing tubs, cooperage and cooling tanks for the water raised from wells located on site. To assemble this complex industrial site it had been necessary to obtain special parliamentary powers especially for authorising the route of the famous vinegar railway line which ran across a public highway. The Vinegar Works became big business, fermenting two million gallons a year. The firm also diversified into making fruit wines which appeared in a variety of wholesome flavours and appealed to that sizeable category of Victorians who did not approve of strong drink.

Industrial chemists were also responsible for the frequent acrid exhalations emerging from the chimneys of Webb and Company situated along the side of the canal at Diglis. Their output of artificial manure contained a highly toxic admixture of constituents like sulphuric acid and animal bone. On occasions the process employed, using aluminium sulphates and calcium super phosphates, must have stunk out whole districts of the City. Webb's also advertised themselves as producers of oil of vitriol and consignees of such pungent soil nutrients as palm nut meal, linseed, cotton seed, and rape cake.

Worcester's lesser known occupations should not be forgotten. Slater's Directory for 1851 lists ten staymakers, twenty-four makers of straw bonnets, four rag and bone dealers and four manufacturers of tarpaulin sheet covers. Also mention were two makers of iron shoe lasts, six cork cutters, and five boat builders. There was a particular local industry we would not expect to find here though it was important enough in its time. Edward Webb's carpet works held on strongly despite the fierce competition from Kidderminster's power looms located just down the road. The business began in 1835 on a site siding onto the Guildhall. Modern jacquard looms were installed in the 1850's and the firm proceeded to build up a sound reputation for hardwearing horsehair rugs which were used by leading railway companies for covering their carriage compartment floors.

One of the most successful of Worcester's late Victorian firms was the mail order business of Kay and Co. The boom in the catalogue company reflected its huge success in the USA and in Britain it was linked to an efficient railway and postal system. Kay's as a company emerged from a prosperous Worcester watchmaking enterprise which had captured big contracts for supplying clocks, watches, and chronometers to the Great Western Railway for whom good timekeeping was almost a sacred duty.

Just along Kay's offices were the works of McNaught and Co. They devoted themselves to the most leisurely and stately form of transport. Their horse drawn carriages complete with associated tackle were the finest in the land. McNaught's became famous for quality materials and craftsmanship of the highest quality in each and every aspect of their production from the bodywork and springs to the wheels and their metal tyres. The vehicle bodywork was carefully primed, painted, varnished, and where appropriate a splendidly executed heraldic device would be applied.

Worcester's numerous trading categories included the manufacture of modern sweet confections. The City Steam Confectionary Works, home of the famous Mother Sigley's sweets, had started up in the 1870's with the aim of satisfying the public demand for cleaner sweet manufacturing conditions. According to Sigley's advertising blurb British sweets had previously been only 'of the commonest kind'. All was now changed and customers were being offered 'the choicest flavours and novelties'. The firm's great speciality was the Mother Sigley Cough Drop – something to help overcome the direst long railway journey and combat that great horror of the Victorian Age, the smog laden fog or 'British particular'. It was a fitting example of Worcester's industrial ingenuity.

WORCESTER ENGINE WORKS

# Drink

'Who'er has travelled life's dull round

Where'er his stages may have been

May sigh to think of how he found

The warmest welcome at an Inn'

William Shenstone, Worcestershire Poet

From *A Wayside Inn*

A good January greeting was to wish everyone 'a happy New Year, a pocket full of money and a cellar full of beer'. In Worcester that could be very strong beer indeed like the local salty mild sold at The Eagle Vaults in Pump Street, reputed to have the second highest specific gravity in England. Other drinkers favoured the quality home brewed ale proudly advertised on the wall of The Hope and Anchor off North Quay and The Albion in Diglis.

But in premises along the canal like the Lame Dog it was likely to be less quaffable. Canal pubs were often regarded as rough places with their greasy wooden settles and battered wooden tables. According to one imbiber they served 'the thinnest and flattest beer I have ever yet come across'. In Worcesterhire ale like that was called 'swanky' or 'swipes' if it had gone really sour. At the King William near the iron foundry in the Blockhouse, they might have followed the Black Country practice of selling 'wobble'– the third 'shut' of the brewing process. Here the ale would be sold by the pailful then taken round to the foundrymen to replace their heavy loss of perspiration.

But any lad coming into Worcester from the countryside was just as likely to be a devotee of cider. Indeed there was a time in neighbouring Herefordshire when three quarts of cider each day was considered part of the wages.

Worcester had always been a city full of pubs but the advent of a new licensing regime dictated that they be exactly classified from the humble alehouses upwards to taverns where spirits could be sold. Above these again were the inns which were obliged by law to provide stabling and shelter. In the lowest category and by far the most numerous were the beerhouses. To obtain a licence, it was only necessary for the landlord to own any property of nominal rateable value and show some sort of passable character reference. In the first rank of licensed premises were the coaching inns: The Hop Pole, The Bell, The Crown and Unicorn, and The Star, or The Star and Garter as it was once known. They served the many fast coaches which used Worcester as a main staging point on the western route from south to north. Bystanders at The Star would view the famously rapid change of horses on the fastest coaches in England. At the rear of the hotel was all the extensive stabling with its bustling crowd of ostlers and grooms. Upstairs was a fine ballroom, rivalling the noble assembly room of the Hop Pole as the venue for grand social occasions and important meetings. In fact The Star was the location for the meeting which launched the Birmingham to Gloucester Railway – a fateful occasion where they brazenly concocted arrangements which would leave Worcester off the railway map for decades.

There was much socialising at these posting houses. We read in Charles Pipe's diary how in the 1880's he became an habitué of the Crown in Broad Street. It was an establishment extensively used by a Worcester Glee Club. Charles Pipe recalls their enjoyable tripe suppers held in the back bar where the drink flowed and as the company mellowed, there would be endless toasts to wives and sweethearts.

Different Worcester pubs tended to attract their own following. Sometimes it would constitute a distinct group of workers or craftsmen. The ironworkers of the Blockhouse gathered in the King William, and the Plough off the Cornmarket was favoured by brushmakers. Some of the pubs were named after particular trades: – the Butchers Arms, Carpenters Arms, Bricklayers Arms, Farriers Arms, Gardeners Arms, Plumbers Arms and the Wheelwrights Arms in Hylton Road. Enthusiasts like herbalists found their refuge at the Green Man, supporters of cock fighting at The Pheasant, showmen and cyclists at the Saracens Head. The Wherry on the Severn waterfront reputedly attracted smugglers. Worcester theatricals famous for their tall stories met up in the Shakespeare which was bang next door to the Theatre Royal. Members of the theatre audience themselves were all to often inebriated. In 1901 their insobriety was bad enough for two constables to be placed up in the 'gods'.

There were also pub names commemorating local aristocratic families who not only owned large tracts of land but held powerful sway on the bench of magistrates. What is now the Cardinal's Hat became the Coventry Arms and there were other licensed houses called after the Vernons, the Berkeleys, the Sebrights and the Berwicks. It had also become the vogue to remember different celebrities and events. The Paul Pry Inn in the Butts took its title from a well known play. There were two pubs named after the battle of Alma in the Crimean War and two more to honour Garibaldi, the famous Italian freedom fighter who was a widely popular hero with the working classes.

Hostelries were the friendly places where you awaited transport back to a neighborouring village. The trade directory for 1806 advertised carrier wagons departing from the Pack horse and in later years they also left from the Old Greyhound (as opposed to the New Greyhound) as well as rolling home from the Reindeer, the Golden Lion, the King's Head, and the Talbot. It was very much the same with water transport and the water ferries which plied their way across the river from the Dog and Duck on the west bank. As for the Severn wherries and barges, they might have set off from the Worcester quayside but their final destination docking was alongside a pub such as the Green Dragon at Bewdley or the Marquis of Granby at Gloucester.

People moved about Britain as never before, and the pub seemed to offer them a break from solitude – a place to find easy company and warmth. Elgar's father coming as an outsider from London was welcomed into the inner circle at the Shades Tavern in Mealchepen Street and later married the landlord's sister, Ann Greening. If it was conversation you desired, hostelries always offered the very best opportunities. Imbibers at the Wherry Inn, for instance, could have availed themselves of discussions with the landlord, George Rogers, an expert craftsman in stained glass with many examples of his workmanship in Worcester and Gloucester Cathedrals. Those in search of political talk would have been drawn to the Golden Lion or the Bull's Head, both facing the Worcester Guildhall. At these pubs the regulars smoked their long pipes and heard the newspapers read out to them. In certain licensed premises the conversation no doubt became dangerously scabrous and in 1888 the local Worcester executioner, 'Hangman Berry', was officially warned off from attending his favourite pub and regaling its clientele with the details of his trade.

## Drunkenness

Worcester hostelries were never lacking in the choice of beverages. Spreckley's Brewery advertised an extensive cellarage of clarets, sherries, burgundies and champagnes, and Stallard's proclaimed for themselves the 'largest collection of vintage ports in the Kingdom'. Spirits were refined at the William's Distillery in the old Turkey district as well as on the premises of The Old Rectifying House near the Worcester Bridge. Some seventeen spirit merchants were mentioned in Stratford's Trade Directory for 1837 – the first year of Victoria's reign – and there were just as many at the time of her death.

The fact that Worcester was visited less drastically than Gloucester in one of the great cholera epidemics, was confidently attributed to its higher consumption of gin. But the hefty degree of local drinking – especially of spirits – began to worry the authorities unduly. In 1848 Mr Davis, the Chief of Police, confessed to The Government's Public Health Inspector, George Clark, his grave concern about the lethal proximity of sixteen large doss houses to all the gin shops near the riverside. The 1848 public health report recorded that 151 drunks had been remanded in custody in the City centre and that according to excise figures, 400 gallons of gin were consumed every week. Police came down most heavily on the pubs where drunkenness was accompanied by gambling and loud music. They used informers to report on pubs which kept open too late and the Worcester City Council Police Watch Committee decided to publish handbills warning about the evils of rat baiting, dog fighting, and other drunken revelries.

The police themselves were not immune from criticism; for in the 1840's constables were still allowed to take their refreshment breaks in beerhouses. The Police Discipline Book for the five year period from 1861-66 showed forty six reprimands for drunkenness, though the main concern of the authorities was of policemen running into debt.

The problem of booze altogether had become a constant worry to Worcester's worthy citizens. Fairs like the old St. John's hiring or mop fair were marked down as a particular source of 'drunkenness and profligacy'. In the 1851 Census of Religious Worship, John Davies, who ran the Episcopal Floating Chapel takes pride that his congregation of boatmen – 'drunkards and blasphemers' 'are becoming new characters'. Crowquill writing in a Berrow's Journal of November 1900 lays into those responsible for the heavy drunkenness on the Severn Steamers. Apparently the inebriation was not confined to passengers. 'There is now', claimed Crowhill 'a tendency to racing among the steamers which is dangerous to the last degree'.

Drunken behaviour at the workplace was now taken seriously. The rules and regulations posted up in 1851 by Chamberlain & Co at the Porcelain Works were completely uncompromising. 'Sobriety' is quoted as indispensable for those wanting permanent work, with swearing and bad language completely forbidden. 'ON NO PRETENCE WHATSOEVER' was any intoxicating drink 'of any description allowed in the Works'.

# Temperance

Powerfully on the Lord's side was the Temperance Movement which in Worcester was a formidable force. It became an organisation empowered by efficiency and a strong sense of missionary passion. One of the leading temperance groups in the land was run from Worcester by the Veteran Grand Templar, Malins. His devotion to the cause arose from his bitter childhood memories of a father who had become ravaged by drink and sold up the family's meagre dwelling. The largest temperance building was in Providence Street with a bold campaigning message displayed on the frontage in elaborately patterned brickwork. 'The blessing of God keep us and protect us from all intoxicating drink'. Temperance was expounded also in other Worcester chapels and mission halls at Pump Street Wesleyan, St. John's Wesleyan, Barbourne Wesleyan, The Primitive Methodists, The Railway Mission, and notably by the Salvation Army with their Saturday night 'Conversion on the Drum' meetings at the top of the Shambles.

Mrs Henry Wood, famed for her perceptive insights, was almost duty bound to deal with the abuse of drink. Her novel, *Danesbury House*, opens with a drink fuddled nurse accidentally administering poison to a nine month old child. Later in the same novel a young mother tragically perishes in a railway accident caused by a drunken gatekeeper.

An interesting solution was to offer the public wholesome and non alcoholic alternatives to the demon drink. In Worcester a few of the pubs were actually closed down and converted into new style coffee lounges which in turn became suitable venues for a number of worthy organisations. In addition two of the city's best known Nonconformists named Hill and Evans, decided to branch out from vinegar manufacture to become Britain's leading suppliers of fruit wines. As a result those 'who signed the pledge' to desist from strong drink could now happily imbibe the pleasurable juices of sweet gooseberry, elderberry and other flavours. All of them had been carefully fermented in Worcester, a city which catered for every taste.

# The Poor

*'All things are dear but poor men's labour'*
(18th-century ballad begun in Worcester)

23 August 1838 in the *Worcester Herald* was a day for bashing radical politicians. According to that newspaper they were 'blasphemy and infamy – the scandal in everything like common decency – the outrage on all morality'. No doubt the real charge was their defence of the poor, a more numerous class than the authorities ever dared to admit.

Many of the poor lived inside the medieval web of central streets, crammed up in courts and rookeried properties like those around the Well of All Hallows or Moreton Court on the site of the old Blackfriar's Cloister or also those further out in the Pinch which housed the descendents of an original cluster community to the west of the old bridge. On the eastern bank it had been decided in the late 18th century to cut a new roadway near the Cathedral in College Street to ease the impossible traffic jam through Sidbury. The result was to leave Lower Friar Street and Lych Street high and dry. Many of their fine old properties became shamefully neglected, and a whole neighbourhood near the Cathedral declined into slums.

Such a swathe of destitution must have created a morbid nervousness in Worcester life generally. Those who could face up to the facts would find them in the 1849 public health report. The Whitehall inspector, George Clark, was sent down to make some kind of sanitary assessment in the wake of a cholera panic. He was not worried about sounding alarmist. – 'A city practically without sewage' he comments – 'pools of liquid filth perpetually stagnate on the surface of the streets there being no adequate drains for their removal'– The report goes on to describe over-flowing graveyards, ineffective water supplies, additional refuse from the numerous slaughterhouses, stables and piggeries and as a highlight – the permanent mountain of manure standing upon Pitchcroft.

Clark, a sound government official in the Benthamite mould, does not spare the detail. We visit the most notorious dosshouses – hotbeds of vice, drunkenness, and crime and learn about the worst of the burial plots: – St Alban's and All Saints where coffins and bodies had become exposed right next to human dwellings. The lowest areas held a macabre fascination for him. He dwells at length on the special problems of St Paul's, the so-called extra parochial district on what was locally known as 'sour ground'. With its jerry built housing in dead straight rows and bad drainage and polluted wells, St Paul's lay outside the official bounds of the city. The inhabitants had no entitlements whatsoever – not even a primitive right of burial – so a corpse could be dumped onto the street awaiting someone who might proffer the kindness of a pauper's funeral.

Sadly the living conditions in this quarter seemed hardly improved thirty-five years later. Henry Douglas, the saintly vicar of St Paul's, showed how his parishioner still lived in grinding poverty, bordering on starvation, and existed in the meanest conditions. Ironically one of the City's hidden memorials was a plaque in All Saints Church to Thomas Malthus. As well as being the brother-in-law to the rector, Malthus was the thinker who frightened respectable opinion into fearing the rate of breeding amongst the poor. In Worcester the population expanded faster, with the exception of certain inner parishes. But not as fast as industrial neighbours like Kidderminster and Dudley.

But who were the worst off? Which people were really at the

bottom of the pile? Could the patients of Worcester's Royal Infirmary have been contenders for such a dubious honour? The hospital was built in the previous century on open fields near Salt Lane and conditions for the poorer patients were hardly ideal. There were frequent outbreaks of erysipelas - a dreadful infection - and on the days they brewed beer in the hospital, clouds of steam came swirling down the ward. One record describes how sick women were woken up at 5:30am to do cleaning duties. Yet, for much of the time this was an establishment with great good will. Sir Charles Hastings expressed it well, describing the Royal Infirmary, as 'the one house of refuge for the infirm and diseased poor'. The numbers of patients were still too few and theorganisation mainly voluntary though by the end of the century there was a special hospital ward for children and an operating theatre fitted out with electricity.

Over the road at the County Jail – where they also took city prisoners – the situation was much worse. The building had been overcrowded from the start; it was intended for 90 but was obliged to accommodate up to 209 prisoners. Inmates at one point included Chartists from the Black Country, those passionate campaigners for the right to vote, who had been banged up as criminals and were vulnerable to all the virulent outbreaks of typhoid and jail fever which raged through the building. As late as 1887 the authorities were forced to call for 'an inquiry of the strictest character' to investigate the precise number of deaths from such prison epidemics.

One more additional misery was the treadmill, worked by eight or ten prisoners. It remained in use until 1901. 'Grinding the air' as someone described it, was intended to reform the character through relentless toil. The mechanism worked in such a way that if any prisoner 'bilked' or eased off, his shins got grazed.

To teach them a salutary lesson inmates might be required to observe any hangings which took place in the execution pit tucked away at the back of the building. And until 1900 any Worcester person involved in a failed suicide bid, would be deemed a criminal offender and liable to end up in this dismal place.

A plan of the jail at the end of the century shows a sizeable female wing with at least one padded cell. Women and poverty were two recurrent themes in local crime. Both the original police station in St Nicholas Street and its successor behind the Guildhall had space for women prisoners with drunkenness and soliciting as two of the more familiar charges. Police had instructions to clear the streets of such problems by ten at night. Worcester was a garrison town so the law enforcement tended to be sharp. Random arrests were common – as with the two lasses summoned before the Police Court in August 1858 for 'brazen insensibility to shame'. Once locked up each prisoner was issued with a metal chamber pot though after 1849 water closets were also available in order 'to abate the cholera'. But for young girls endangered by prostitution there was some real hope of rescue at the Female Asylum in Landsdown Crescent – a local version of a London magdelan with its own medical advisor. It appeared to offer a regime of positive instruction and training in needlework and domestic crafts.

Whether justly or not, severe policing was viewed as an effective way of dealing with poverty. Police activity was always a priority with a superintendent, five sergeants, and twenty five constables on the pay roll in 1873 and more spent on the police budget than in comparable cities like Exeter. Magistrates courts frequently dealt out strict sentences for minor misdemeanours. The *Berrows Journal* of January 1879 for example reported the case against

Joseph Bird, Charles Williams, and John Williams hauled up for the heinous crime of sliding on the ice in College Street. In June 1902 the unfortunate individual in the dock was Mary Jones who was accused of stealing threepence worth of rag and iron off the Corporation tip in the Moors. Anyone drunk, scruffy and dirty might find himself branded an incorrigible criminal. Daniel McCarry for example was described in a newspaper of November 1861 as being drunk and disorderly and also being 'a butty and fellow lodger of the famous old Gomersky, so notorious for raw head and bloody bones business'.

The main institution after 1834 for coping with grinding poverty was the workhouse, serving the administrative area of the Worcester Poor Law Union and capable of accommodating up to 1,500. Byfield's late 18th-century classical building had originally been known as the House of Industry but it then came under the strict control of the centralised body of the Poor Law Commissioners, popularly known as the 'Bashaws of Somerset House'. Though certain powers were reserved for locally elected guardians, the workhouse was mainly regulated harshly by a highly centralised regime bent on encouraging people to stay away. 'Her's gone up the Hill' comments a character of Mrs Henry Wood on some unfortunate female who had been admitted to the Tallow Hill 'spike'. The workhouse was indeed a sad place though, according to Mr Wheale, one of the Poor Law Commissioners, its purpose was not oppressing the poor but merely 'to teach them that pauperism was a degradation'. One problem was the mixing together of different inmates: with children accommodated alongside adults and until Powick Asylum was built, mental patients were bundled in with all the rest. An especially poignant case was that of William Nionent aged 13, described in the 1847 lunacy return as 'not dangerous and not dirty but an idiot'. Visiting the workhouse children's ward in the 1880's was something which greatly upset Charlie Pipe, Elgar's brother-in-law, just after he had been congratulating himself on becoming a Poor Law Guardian.

There were fierce arguments in Worcester about Workhouse conditions. In 1838 a letter in Berrows newspaper from a Mr Bowen – waxed angry about the official diktat which refused to permit relatives smuggling in a small gift of tea or sugar for elderly inmates. 'Are we brought to this pass in Christian England?' he demanded. Protests were still rumbling on in the 1890's. In November 1894 a request from the inmate, Thomas Morgan, for variations to his diet on medical grounds, was flatly refused. The same guardian's board meeting decided upon the case of a Catholic inmate asking to be served fish on Fridays – a request which was dismissed as 'ridiculous'. Just a few years later, the chairman of the board of guardians was advocating much sterner measures for vagrants who were described as 'men who preferred to lead a roving life instead of a hard-working and honourable one'. It was seen as a problem serious enough for introducing labour colonies in every county where 'they could be taught to adopt 'industrious habits'.

If the workhouse was dreaded so was the unemployment which landed you there. Worcester slumps were not quite so bad as those in Kidderminster where in 1851 a crisis in the carpet trade drove off a quarter of the town's population. But unfortunately in Worcester some categories of employment were barely above subsistence level like match sellers, sweeps, scavengers, cads (or those ready to run cheap errands). To avoid begging, a smart move was taking out a peddlers licence which for 5 shillings a year allowed you to sell matches or bootlaces – with the hope that purchasers might throw in some additional small change. All too often unemployment hit Worcester's biggest industry – that of gloving. The two large manufactures Dents and Fownes employed many male hands as well as an army of female gloveresses on outwork – time consuming and indifferently paid. The Operative Glovers Society which was a trades union did their best for 'the relief of members out of employment'. But gloving was altogether too volatile with the new machines, the changes in fashion, greater competition, and the readiness of foreign countries to slap on protective trade tariffs at a moment's notice.

Even in a genteel trade like porcelain there was little long term security. R W Binns, the best type of Victorian general manager, kept Worcester Royal afloat by new designs, technical innovations, and a restless search for new markets. General economic changes meant some occupations disappearing altogether. These included the watermen and the bowhauliers who had pulled craft along the riverbank and the roaring gangs of navvies who left town after the major spate of railway construction. By the end of the century the knife was turning on skilled machinists working at the Vulcan – their jobs now being undermined by the new type of machine tools imported in from the USA – some quite likely from the factories of Worcester, Massachusetts.

The poor were sometimes hit by some freakish act of nature. The great flood of 1886 brought misery to the occupants of many low lying dwellings. In 1901 it would be something different – the rhinepest or swinefever which attacked the surrounding farms, bringing with it inevitable hardship for many Worcester traders.

Bad standards of health added greatly to the general poverty. The early career of that great doctor, Charles Hastings, shows the sheer enormity of the medical task. During the cholera crisis, we find him exhorting families from low-lying hovels in the central districts to get away and bivouac up on the higher ground at Ronkswood. Hastings was also involved in a running battle with the City Council to improve public health and had deep concerns about the occupational hazards of certain Worcestershire industries. He identified that the porcelain workers were suffering from the toxic effects of lead glazes and those in the gloving trade from noxious processes such as using urine to treat the leather skins.

So underlying the apparent Trollopian calm of the Cathedral City there were less salubrious layers. It was difficult for destitute people to speak up for themselves, so the voice of the poor was not always heard. For that reason alone we should treasure scarce quotations like this one from the 1906 parliamentary enquiry into political corruption. The unemployed defendant, cross examined by an eminent barrister, was trying to justify his acceptance of a monetary bribe to go and vote. Why did he do it? 'I was', claimed the defendant, 'low in pocket' – after long bouts out of work and in constant fear of the work-house. 'I went hop picking that's the best I done. What money I saved from hop picking helped to keep us'.

Well intentioned individuals were not indifferent to such problems. Mrs Henry Wood was invariably sympathetic – closely observing poverty in its many different forms. Richard Mitchell aged ten, one of seven malnourished children is portrayed in the story *Mildred Arkell* as dying outdoors in the bitter cold. In Pomeroy Abbey three babies die in a single family. A much lesser writer, Charlie Pipe confided to his diary his troubled feelings at discovering the depth of – 'heartrending' poverty in the crowded housing courts off King Street just a stone's throw from the Cathedral. It was no wonder that in Worcester there were at least four agents dealing with emigration to the USA and the colonies.

Providing solutions was never going to be easy. There would

always be a minority quick to condemn. 'What shall we do with the unemployed?' queried the sarcastic commentator in the *Worcester Sauce Magazine* of December 23rd 1886. 'offer them free refreshments at all city pubs from 6 am to 11 pm and erect loungers' rests at the street corners?' We have already noted the heavy emphasis on law enforcement. The authorities were on constant look-out for any outbreaks of popular violence as in neighbouring Kidderminster where relations between local carpet workers and immigrant Irish farm labourers could get very nasty. The Worcester police were clearly anxious to avoid similar incidents when that familiar local greeting 'I'll warm yer nut' (punch your head) could signal the beginning of a major punch-up.

There were other suspects too. The 1887 edition of the *Worcester Saurce* warned of 'filthy vagabonds that infect our riverbanks in the evenings'. Fortunately those with influence were also looking for more constructive solutions. Worcester's first Medical Officer of Health, Dr William Strange, was a specialist in medical statistics having earned extensive public health experience in the North. He drew attention to the raw figures – and raw they were, with an abnormally high incidence of child mortality from scarlet fever and diphtheria. Only in 1894 were the financial objections swept aside and filter beds installed for dealing with the seriously tainted drinking water. There was also mounting official pressure about tackling the poor quality and inadequate popular housing. To guard against bad times, people devised their own forms of insurance. 19th-century Worcester possessed a range of friendly societies including branches of the Oddfellows, the Buffaloes and others who met in rooms above pubs and down alleyways. Their sessions were characterised by cheerful, quirky, ceremonial, and secret oaths. The rules for regulating the Provident Friendly Society of

Married and Single Women meeting at The Duke of Wellington in 1824, stipulated that dues were to be paid into a strong box with the keys held by 'Mother' and her two junior club officers known as 'Matrons'. After twelve months a sick woman was entitled to five shillings benefit when out of work, and for any funeral members were ordered to attend with their white gloves and a posy or nosegay. By 1880 the friendly societies movement in the City was sufficiently established to possess its own Worcester Amalgamated Friendly Societies Medical Assocation with offices in Foregate Street and the services of its own medical officer.

Help from different institutions became slightly more systematic and organised. In 1842 Henry Hebb, a former mayor, made it his task to rationalise and classify local grant aiding bodies and charities to counter accusations of malpractice. Benevolence could help to alleviate poverty but was sometimes administered uncharitably. Sir Thomas Whyte's Charity enjoined that benefits should be removed automatically when any applicant was guilty 'of insobriety, insubordination, breach of regulations or immoral or improper conduct'. So poor people desiring aid, were wise to look respectable. Worthy citizens often raised money through their churches and chapels and the Worcester Royal Infirmary began providing free ophthalmic services at Castle Street with a limited amount of free dental surgery and advice at No 10 Friar Street.

During the last twenty years of Victoria's reign workers confronted serious economic difficulty. Industrial competition pushed engineering employers like the Vulcan into taking a hard line. The local branch of the ASE union found piecework forced upon them and were locked out from work if they tried to resist. Worcester unions had achieved quite passable credentials; this area for instance was one of the first five branches of Robert Owen's pioneering Grand National Consolidated Trades Union and local gloveworkers were involved in the famous Chartist Land Plan which set up pioneering agricultural settlements at Dodford and Snigg's End (then in Worcestershire) during the 1840's. Yet by the 1890's despite the work of the Worcester Trades Council, it looked as if unionism could not advance further without direct involvement in politics. Times had changed.

The one bright spot was the Coop, which only started after the second attempt but quickly into its stride. In Worcester the Coop was the very model of working class self-help. Members were offered more than good solid retailing. There were saving schemes to help housewives, party fun and choirs for children as well as women's guilds and wide ranging education schemes with training in self- government through the Coop committees. On December 14th, 1898 the grand new central premises were opened with an extravaganza of speeches and high tea. What had begun with a capital of £79 in 1881, was now achieving sales of £347,958. Mr Manning, the Coop Treasurer and seasoned campaigner for the 9 hour working day, stressed that the occasion was about more than some fine new retail buildings. The Coop, he declaimed, was about helping 'their fellow creatures into a higher and better position socially and morally'. – 'The Society was a 'monument to the industry of the working man'.

# Worcester's 'Well To Do'

'Oh England is a pleasant place for them that's rich and high'
[Charles Kingsley : *The Last Buccaneer* (1858)]

We remember how George III, faced with the threat of invasion from revolutionary France, considered that loyal dependable Worcestershire might prove his best source of refuge should the worst come to the worst. Years later in 1837 when Queen Victoria came to the throne, the county town still bore clear hallmarks of the old regime. Worcester's principal motto proclaimed it to be 'the faithful city'. The message was emblazoned on the gates of the Guildhall, a building with links to civic authority stretching back to 1249.

Decidedly amongst the upper class were certain members of the Anglican higher clergy. The last of the socially grand bishops was William Carr, a court favourite of George IV. After his death predatory creditors caused so much trouble, his successor, Bishop Pepys, decided to go and live at Hartlebury Castle, a truly congenial gentleman's property well out of town. It was a bad move – Hartlebury was inconveniently located and expensive to run, and the bishop's absences made him socially a more remote figure to Worcester people.

Into the Old Palace moved Dean Peel whose new deanery was located bang next door to the smoking bottle kilns of a busy tile manufactory. But it was still an address of some status, and since Dean Peel was the wealthy brother of the prime minister, he enjoyed unquestionable social standing in the city. The diary of a young cathedral chorister, James Smith, portrays a somewhat deferential impression of life in the remainder of the Cathedral

Close. For him the striking cathedral figures from his early life were mostly those from an aristocratic background. There was the Reverend the Hon. John Fortescue, 3rd son of Earl Fortescue occupant of stall number 5 followed by Canon John Ryce Wood occupant of stall number 8 – 'equally distinguished and courtly in different ways'. Canon Wood had once been chaplain to Queen Adelaide and a tutor to one of the royal dukes. It was claimed that sometimes when leaving a room he walked backwards until he reached the door – apparently a courtly mannerism acquired in earlier years. At the time of the 1881 census, his age was given as 74 and his household at 11 College Green comprised a butler, Abraham Barrs, a page, Edwin Loyes, a domestic housekeeper, a housemaid, and two maids to care for the two ladies in residence.

## The Landowning Influence

Without doubt the influence of county landowners remained strong in Worcester where they continued to make many of the key decisions, as property owners and magistrates. And for a long time many essential services were provided under private act of parliament. by 'improvers' who were just the gentry under another name.

For a brief period the tenant of the large Great Witley estate was the Dowager Queen Adelaide who left in 1846 to the regret of the local populace - especially the tradesmen. Of delicate health and unable to walk far, she travelled about in her carriage, and as leader of county society came to Worcester for theatrical visits. In his autobiographical sketches, George Griffiths describes how large numbers of local people who had deliberately journeyed out to obtain a glimpse of the Queen were afterwards overcharged by a morose landlord of the Hundred House Inn who made excessive profits from supplying refreshments.

The widest of the rolling acres around Worcester belonged to the Earl of Coventry at Croome Court. The family had risen due to their prowess as sharp lawyers and recorders of the City of Worcester. By the accession of Queen Victoria, however, the title was in a crisis. The heir apparent, Lord Deerhurst, known in the popular press as 'the simpleton Deerhurst' died young from consumption aggravated by a severe chill – the remedy he had been prescribed 'powdered sqills, ginger grains potash and orange peel' being drastically unsuccessful. The 8th Earl himself was to die in 1843 from 'an unsound mind' after embroiling himself in long, acrimonious political disputes over the Corn Laws. The turmoil of his personal life was demonstrated in 1840 at a Conservative dinner in the Guildhall, Worcester where he was handed an anonymous letter accusing him of being 'an outcast from society and a disgrace to his coronet'. As it happened the Worcester Journal would be even more unkind to his son-in-law, Colonel Coventry, who died soon after him :

> 'Here lies Mr Crawford to moulder and rot
> Who married Lord Coventry's daughter
> And always was known by the name of Teapot
> From being so much in hot water'

The 9th Earl succeeded in 1843 at five years old and came of age in February 1858 with a large banquet at the Guildhall. He lived long, cultivating throughout his life the role of the quintessential country gentleman. He had many excuses for dropping into Worcester. He was a leading magistrate and acted as nominal head of the Tory Party in the county, although he could hardly be described as strenuous in his pursuit of politics. He was convinced of his duty to defend agriculture which was the mission passed on from his immediate predecessor, who had spoken at the Guildhall, more than once to rally support for the Corn Laws. Two of Lord Coventry's most imaginative projects came to nothing: – agricultural credit banking which had been a great success in Germany and might have been a boon to local small holders. And secondly the idea of a light railway running into Worcester from Upton which would certainly have benefited the rural economy but which required a much more sustained and competent financial management than he seemed capable of providing.

When the Worcestershire County Council was formed, Lord Coventry's seniority made him an automatic choice, and he served for forty years as a county member before handing over to a close relative.

Worcester newspapers often alluded to Lord Coventry's pleasures:– his horses, hounds, Herefords, and cricket. His prestigious Hereford herd begun in 1875 contributed towards elevating the breed as a serious competitor to Shorthorn cattle. There was even an occasional adventure in this healthy outdoor lifestyle. Out hunting on horseback in the late 1860's, the Earl and Countess both plunged headlong, thirty feet into a quarry. And in 1873 he was left dangling twenty feet in the air after his grandstand seat at Cheltenham Racecourse collapsed beneath him.

The ancestors of Frederick, 6th Earl Beauchamp, had been the powerful royal sheriffs controlling 13th-century Worcester. In late Victorian times Earl Beauchamp still held considerable sway. He was Lord Steward of the royal household for six years and was one of England's leading high churchmen in a period when such views though risky were increasingly fashionable.

Politically the 6th Earl was high Tory, and in 1865 was singled out for mention by Disraeli for his 'resolution and energy' in the important electoral battle which unseated Gladstone in Parliament. Here clearly was the very man to build up support in Worcester and Worcestershire during a period of marked growth in party politics. And when county councils came into being in 1888, we find Earl Beauchamp personally responsible for nominating each one of the county aldermen, a sizeable group who were appointed not elected. As we saw when meetings started, these were seated on a specially elevated dais over and above all the rest.

Earl Beauchamp was appointed to a number of important parliamentary commissions looking into child welfare, education, and local government. His wide connections brought him into contact with the work of Florence Nightingale, and he pushed hard to get her new nursing techniques adopted at Worcester's Royal Infirmary where he was Chairman of the Board. His interest in education stimulated him, along with Canon Butler to establish Britannia House as the City's first private girls school with Miss Alice Ottley as its formidable headmistress.

Even before Queen Adelaide's departure, the Great Witley estate had been purchased for a record price of £890,000 by the trustees of William Humble Ward. In 1860 he became the Earl of Dudley having already inherited a large fortune based on Black Country industry. Even when profits dipped somewhat in the 1880's, it hardly diminished the impact of Dudley wealth and influence.

Lord Dudley's involvement in the Cathedral restoration became a cause célèbre in Victorian Worcester but less was known about his offer to stump up the cash for rescuing the Arboretum as a public open space – a generous gesture spurned by the authorities.

Command of the local yeomanry, the Queen's Own Worcestershire Hussars, was a matter very close to his heart. No doubt being colonel-in-chief reminded him of earlier times when aristocracy wielded more clout, and when the yeomanry were the ultimate policing power. It was certainly true that the fortunes of the yeomanry benefited from a patron of such wealth. For it was Lord Dudley who paid up for all the saddlery and for the expensive officers' uniforms. His social standing and influence also allowed him to exert pressure in the right places to keep Pitchcroft as an open space for military exercises and drilling.

The Great Witley estate with its army of servants and hundreds of horses was bound to be good for local trade. The immense scale of the rebuilding and landscaping under Samuel Daukes and William Nesfield inevitably brought business to local firms and contractors like Forsyths, the sculptors. By the 1890's Witley Court had become a favoured location for the Prince of Wales who descended with his own retinue staff in preparation for lavish parties and big shoots. The residents of Worcester remained bemused and must have followed these royal comings and goings with endless fascination, wondering all the while why the Prince found no reason to drop into town.

The fourth Lord Lyttleton, residing at Hagley, was regarded as an exemplary Victorian patrician aristocrat. In the 1860's he was an education commissioner who became identified with the policy changes to all secondary schools including those of Worcestershire. Being the brother-in-law of Prime Minister Gladstone, he was clearly a man of influence and demonstrated this in 1862 by his involvement in the urgent task of restoring the Cathedral. And as head of a passionate cricketing family, he was a prime mover in forming a Worcestershire County Cricket Club – formally inaugurated at a meeting in the Star Hotel in 1865.

These were times of change and the gentry were hardly inclined to relax their hold easily - least of all their strong powers as magistrates sitting in the quarter sessions. Predictably therefore the Chairman of the old quarter sessions, Sir John Pakington, would become closely involved in setting up Worcestershire's new county constabulary whose headquarters were based within the City. Pakington's 'one nation' approach made him an ideal person to oversee its inauguration - it also prompted his interest in workers' self education and the creation of a Worcester workingmen's institute.

## Trade Creeps In

Money counted and local gentry were not immune from commercial interests. As the market for housing expanding rapidly, their sizeable parcels of town land rocketed in value, and it was not by chance that many new streets bore the names of historic families like Somers, Vernons, Berwicks and Sebrights.

Those involved in commerce and manufacture, despite their rugged independence, were sometimes drawn by the lure of gentility. For instance when Worcester Royal Porcelain was clambering out of slump in 1865, they were happy to secure a specially prestigious order which would show off the firm's brilliant capabilities in craftsmanship and design. The sale item in question was a jewelled tea set with wondrously beautiful Raphael-like panels painted by Thomas Callowhill. The customer was the Corporation of Worcester, intent on pleasing the new Countess of Dudley with a stunning wedding present.

Lea and Perrins Worcestershire Sauce owed part of their success to ingeniously clever advertising*. Their early marketing ploy

*See Victorian Specialities for more detail.

was to claim that the sauce's famous secret recipe had reputedly been brought from India 'by a nobleman of Worcestershire'. It was understood that the nobleman in question had been a high ranking official in the province of Madras; one of the 'Sandys of Ombersley' whose elite delicacy could now be made available to the public at large. It was a splendid story but the fact was – no member of the Sandys family had lived in Madras or India.

Gloving was Worcester's most historic trade with its manufacturers always playing a prominent part in running the City. John and William Dent had been identified with the old unreformed governance of Worcester, but in 1837 they attempted a move upwards by purchasing the Tudor royal residence of Sudeley in Gloucestershire. There they lived in style, finally passing on the estate to their nephew, John Coucher Dent. By this time he was more country gentleman than industrialist. It showed in July 1881 when a group of Dents factory employees were invited over to Sudeley for a tour of inspection. Bowled over by their experience they returned home and subsequently drew up a deferential address of gratitude elaborately composed and illustrated. 'A trifling souvenir of our visit' as they modestly described it.

The social boundary between trade and blue blood was one topic which intrigued Worcester's best known Victorian novelist, Mrs Henry Wood, a convinced believer in good breeding. She addresses the theme of corrupting trade in her story *Trevlyn Hold* where the young heir to a landed estate is cheated out of his inheritance and compelled to earn his living as a shop hand. 'A slender handsome boy with earnest eyes and chestnut hair, he had to stand behind the counter and unroll goods and measure tapes and ribbons and say Sir and Madam.'

Aspiring new landowners grounded in trade must have found some difficulties in 'living it up'. That was certainly so if they were attempting to model themselves on the lifestyle of Lord and Lady Northwick. The family resided just outside Worcester at Northwick Park together with their famed art collections and elegant fern gardens. Selected visitors were welcomed round and encouraged to linger awhile at the gravestone of an ancient trout which had been laid to rest on 29th April 1855 at the age of twenty.

The test of social acceptability was invariably applied. Some passed easily like the Allsops, leading members of the 'beerocracy' whose fortunes rested on that favoured Victorian tipple, Ind Coope and Allsop, Burton Ale. Lord Hindlip, head of the family, resided at Hindlip Hall, and in 1884 his son was politically powerful enough to seize the local parliamentary seat from its Liberal sitting member, Alderman Hill.

Businessmen and industrialists on their way up the social ladder would be anxious to make their mark. Alexander Clunes Sheriff, Worcester's railway baron, bought up the Perdiswell estate. His pathway to respectability involved election as the local MP and mayor on two separate occasions. His gift to the Corporation of Worcester of massive mayoral chains (styled of course in the form of railway couplings), was clearly intended to convey a message – that grandeur and the trappings of power were no longer confined to the favoured few.

## Respect Must be Shown

What would strike us most were we transported back? The costumes? The smells? Possibly even stranger – the ostentatious degree of respectful deference which had to be accorded to those classified as 'important'. The General Police Order in late

Victorian times laid down strict instructions that significant citizens must always be saluted by the constabulary – most especially The Mayor, Deputy Mayor, Magistrates and each member of the Watch Committee.

This was very much a world where appearances mattered. How could you be important if you didn't look important? It was an opinion passionately endorsed by the owners of The City and County Laundry in Barbourne, who claimed that social status was judged by the superiority of a person's linen. The firm boasted their prowess in general laundry, including table napery 'which would be got up in faultless style' and delivered to the home 'in well appointed vans'. The sparkle of the starch must always involve the expenditure of great effort! All their laundry-work', they argued was performed by hand'. Chemicals and injurious materials were taboo – in favour of 'good old fashioned soap, soda and starch and plenty of elbow grease'. The elbow grease, we assume , was supplied by those of a lesser social order.

# Building Up Worcester

Sometimes it was just a question of knocking things down. In the 1880's they demolished the Old Trinity Hall with some of its 14th-century neighbours in order to cut through a new street. Twenty or so years before they had removed the ancient charnel house chapel standing hard up against the house opposite the Cathedral North Porch this time to provide a grander and securer entrance into Deanery Yard.

But the citizens were well aware that their City was in a phase of rapid physical development right across the range from prestigious public buildings to small terrace houses. Next to the Cathedral the most significant candidate for restoration was Thomas White's famous 18th-century Guildhall which started exhibiting ominous cracks in the 1860's. Some members of the Corporation saw here the opportunity for a new town hall like the one in Manchester and worthy of modern 19th-century aspirations. It provoked Sir Gilbert Scott, leading architect of his time, to issue a serious warning. Worcester, he claimed, was earning itself 'unenviable notoriety'. Fortunately the Corporation withdrew their option to demolish, inviting Scott himself to participate in an extensive restoration exercise – particularly of the Assembly Room which emerged refurbished after a lush Italianate make-over.

The Cathedral restoration itself was a wonder of the age, phased over three decades and according to the authoritative *Builder* magazine costing more than any comparable scheme. A number of significant architects were involved: Abraham Perkins, Ewart Christian, and Sir Gilbert Scott, and craftsmen of the highest calibre to deal with the fabric, stained glass, rood screen, pulpit, font, woodwork, and other interior features. But when Forsyth, Brock, Hardman, Bodley, and other artist craftsmen had completed their task – was the outcome not a trifle exuberant? The undertaking certainly caused arguments. The famous authority Ruskin was unkindly critical, believing the venture was excessive. Better a building to end up a stately ruin like Tintern or Rievaulx, he suggested 'than the fate of Worcester or Durham'. In 1846 the decision was taken to use the Old Palace as a permanent deanery even though Dean Peel was not keen about residing there, and the new Bishop secretly desired to move back from his over-spacious accommodation at Hartlebury Castle. But matters went ahead. The building was adapted, utilising material from former prebendal houses, and with fewer canons in residence, College Green now attained more the aspect of a cathedral close.

As we have noted, new churches sprang up all over the suburbs, and many ancient ones like St Nicholas and All Saints were being refurbished. Frederick Preedy, that most prolific of local architects, had overall twenty new churches to his name and thirty major restorations. In Worcester he built the new churches at St Mary's in the Arboretum, St Clement's, and St Stephen's, Barbourne, and was the keen patron of George Rogers the Worcester stained glass maker. Sir Aston Webb, an architect of national repute, married the daughter of a local doctor and accordingly won several commissions in the area. His design for St George's in Barbourne was inspired by St George's Chapel Windsor with a recessed western wall, a bold arch, and imaginative brickwork. Earlier in 1888, at Angel Street Congregational Chapel, Webb had also made highly effective use of brick in constructing a large Sunday school complex on a difficult corner site. His courageous design was a fitting addition to the original chapel built in 1859 to a deliberately classical Roman style no doubt to provide some contrast to the prevalent Anglican vogue for gothic. Over on the other side of town Catholics were about this time enhancing their original church with a fine stone façade, lady chapel, and elaborate ironwork in the manner of 19th-century papal Rome.

Worcester was no Liverpool, replete with the wealth of empire, but there was prosperity enough to afford buildings of a certain grandeur. The Royal Albert Orphanage erected along the Henwick Road in 1869 boasted a neo-Venetian gothic frontage and there were further elaborations to follow. The Victoria Institute, devised as combined museum, art gallery, library, and school, was executed in an animated mixture of the Tudor and the baroque using building materials of terracotta and shining red brick. Such confidence and flamboyance contrasted sharply with the modest good taste of the classical Greek style of the Shire Hall next door which after 1888 became the official residence of the Worcestershire County Council as well as the County Assizes. A chastely classical design had also been chosen for two of the public market halls: the Corn Exchange erected in 1848 for supporters of the Corn Law and the General Market opposite the Guildhall – described in *Bentley's Directory of 1840* as 'a beautiful stone front, being surmounted by an ornamental and panelled square pediment supported by handsome Tuscan columns'. But the Hop Market Buildings belonged to a different age. They were constructed in 1900 of red brick and terracotta and by Worcester standards were quite massive. Like the new Coop retail emporium round the corner in St Nicholas Street they involved squeezing every ounce of development onto a cramped site. Almshouses and hospitals too were being extended and expanded along with all the rest. St Oswald's was refurbished for its elderly residents in 1874, and new almshouses were built for the St Nicholas Charity along Infirmary Walk. Much agonising took place over possible developments at The Royal Infirmary in Castle Street. After extensions in 1823 there was still a chronic shortage of the most basic facilities; surgical and medical patients were located in the same ward with no 'operating room'. Further building took place in 1849, and by 1871 an architect had been commissioned to investigate the possibilities of an outpatients' department, a separate laundry, and accommodation for the nurses. Of great concern to the worthies of Worcester was the lack of a special hospital chapel. In 1851 sufficient subscriptions were raised under the patronage of the famous operatic soprano, Jenny Lind 'the Swedish Nightingale'. But no sooner it was built than the criticism began about some decidedly non liturgical activities taking place within. Pressures on available space meant that the small attached room familiarly known as 'the crypt' was allocated to the house surgeon whilst a confined area underneath the chapel became a place for drying bed linen. When Worcester gained its first municipal cemetery, it was obligatory once again to provide a special chapel. In the end they erected two mortuary chapels; one for the Anglicans, the other for Nonconformists.

The 19th-century municipality at last faced up to its responsibility for investing in water and drainage schemes. The sums were considerable and definite; financial limits were imposed. The engineer chosen was Thomas Hawksley whose highly ambitious plan at Leicester allowed a plentiful supply of water to be piped from Thornton, nine miles to the north. This level of expense was far too drastic for Worcester and the new Barbourne Waterworks along the bank of the Severn though impressive technically was built with a distinct eye to economy. The water drawn up by steam driven pumps was then passed through a series of sand filters and settlement tanks. But because of the cost, main filters were not introduced until 1894. This was despite the consequences to health in a city well known for its typhoid and its dire reputation for scarlet fever and diphtheria. A different project underwritten by government funding was the construction of the large barracks just outside the City at Norton in 1876. Worcester was always a garrison town; even more so now that a major portion of the County regiment could be housed within those red brick battlements.

By this time Worcester possessed a large gas works off Rainbow Hill with two gasometers, and there was now so much smoke stack industry that the city was officially compared with big northern towns for its smog problems. The vogue had decidedly begun for impressive commercial and industrial premises. Most prestigious architecturally were the banks, and the most pretentious was E W Elmslie's Worcester City and County Bank – four bays wide and ashlar faced with a portal of marble columns – 'the provincial bank at its most confidence-inspiring', as Nicholas Pevsner describes it. Its imposing presence was important in a City where a serious bank failure threatened financial disaster for so many, as in the collapse of Farley's Bank in 1857 which was traumatic enough to be borrowed by Mrs Henry Wood in her novel – *The Shadow of Ashlydat*.

The river and canal trade encouraged and boosted building along the towpath with new locks and workshops at Diglis and other buildings like Townshends Flour Mill, large and looming alongside the Porcelain Factory. A number of the finest new buildings were constructed in brick. It was very much the fashionable medium especially since Worcester now possessed a large new brickworks erected in Gregory's Bank by D W Barker which utilised the latest in German kiln-fired technology. A notable edifice in patent brick was the filling house of the Hill Evans Vinegar Works with vats containing up to 20,000 gallons.

Over across from this great brick hall at Shrub Hill, was the Worcester Engine Works described in *The Illustrated Midland News* of November 6th 1869 as 'a handsome substantial building constructed under the supervision of Mr Edward Wilson, an engineer of great eminence'.

The Shrub Hill Railway Station, not far away, had been necessarily conceived as another economy project. Its reconstruction in 1865 was accomplished more boldly using an Italianate style in dark engineering brick with the ladies room on Platform 2, glazed in Maw's Jackfield Tiles, offering a delightfully extravagant feature. The opening of the Hereford Line meant that the station was approached via the exceptionally splendid brick viaduct passing high over the Arboretum.

The Worcester Royal Porcelain Company had their own ambitious plans for expanding into the Arboretum with a new manufactory complete with impressive curved brick façade. When unfortunately the finances collapsed, it was decided to lessen this grandeur and settle for a cheap solution. The new building scheme was speedily and expeditiously crammed onto land still available at the old Chamberlain's site.

In a great age of house building, Joseph Wood's big yard, centrally positioned in the Butts, underlined the significance of the town's principal contractor. The woodworking side was described as 'an industrial department', proudly advertising its sawing, planing, and moulding mills with their immense stocks of valuable woods stored up for seasoning. A firm like Osborne and Sharpe could supply every variety of paint and plumbing requirements as well as offering an impressive selection of 'glass plate, sheet and crown glass, ornamental, patent plate, rough rolled, rolled and cast plate glass, glass slates, tiles, silvered glass, glass shades and louvre ventilators'.

Worcester building styles often followed the London fashion. Properties in Field Terrace in the early 1850's were faced in cement, coloured and jointed just like those recently built in Kensington and some of the imposing new residences in Barbourne, Battenhall, and St John's had picturesque architectural flourishes worthy of London's Bedford Park. Richer residents decided where possible to live away from the dust and disease. Britannia Square and St George's Square were two early examples of this select development. But Mount Battenhall, Worcester's most ambitious adventure in domestic architecture, was not constructed until the 1890's.

The supply of small basic houses was hindered not helped by the influential Local Government Act of 1858 introducing rigid new bye laws. Details of building and drainage proposals for any kind of new development had henceforth to be submitted to the Corporation. It might signify an improving quality of construction for better class housing, but the cost of the exercise was passed on in the form of higher rents all round. Many poorer folk were forced into the multi-occupation of derelict, old, city centre properties or into inadequate dwellings built on odd scraps of land.

Behind this keen demand for less sumptuous housing was the rapid expansion of the local population. City lawyers who knew a thing or two, linked up with builders to carve up the extensive grounds surrounding many of the old properties. The process is clearly illustrated when we look at the former estate of Francis Williams at Henwick Grange in St John's. After coming up for auction in 12 lots at The Star Hotel on June 24th, 1875, they were then sold on to different purchasers for smaller plots for building houses or villas. One of the business participants was John Rouse, the Lowesmoor stonemason who was building all over town. He worked closely with John Stallard, the solicitor, in a mutually advantageous relationship. Rouse, often strapped for ready money, needed help with his cash flow and a facility was provided for arranging mortgages through the Worcester Building Society over which John Stallard held control. Other facilities also required construction. By the 1890's large tracts of land off London Road were filling up with new housing so fast it was necessary to build a new district school at Red Hill, modelled on the one put up just a year previously at Cherry Orchard.

The prevalence of bad housing in the town pricked the social conscience of local reformers. The backs of Worcester's ancient burgage plots had become crammed with in-filled overcrowded housing courts, and long lines of cheap speculative housing had been constructed on undrained land left over after the canal was cut through the Extra Parochial District of St Paul's. Many larger old properties in areas like Lych Street had been divided into tenements before steadily declining into slums.

Deeply engrossed with the problem was William Strange, Worcester's first Medical Office of Health. He was an outstanding medical professional faced with a virtually impossible task. His appointment had been forced by new statutory requirements, and he set about his work task reinforced by his impressive medical qualifications and a wealth of public health experience in northern towns. Strange had a deep knowledge of new statistical methods which could now be applied and was author of an important treatise *Seven Sources of Health* (1864). He concluded that there was a direct causal connection between the average incidence of certain epidemics and Worcester's serious lack of living space. His voice was welcomed in the push for more housing to rent particularly accommodation with more than a single bedroom. Already in 1855 there had been a useful experiment with the opening of so called Model Dwellings in Copenhagen Street – initially a scheme for nine dwellings along the lines of similar schemes in London. The aim was worthy enough – in the words of *The Worcester Journal* 'to effect permanent results sanitary and moral'. Unfortunately the charity organization backing it up could not be sustained. In 1878 the association was abruptly wound up; after which the initiative lay with private builders and developers alone. Their efforts are still with us in the many streets like Stanley Road off Wylde's Lane, constructed of solid brick with fancy machine carving over the porch and bearing house names resonant of Victorian Empire:– Jameson Villa and Pretoria Villa. Suddenly in those last years of Victoria's reign, Worcester had become a bigger place.

# Schooling

'The School Board also bless
O, May their work progress
God bless our school.
May education's power
Help in temptation's hour
The young who are their dower
God bless our school'
(The Worcester School Board Anthem of the 1890's)

## Even Workhouse Children Must be Schooled

In Victorian times kindness or fear convinced the authorities it was time to allow more schooling for the poor. This even included the workhouse children at Tallow Hill who were provided with their own schoolmaster. The residents of the rambling Gothic Royal Albert Orphanage in St John's, Worcester, were also required to receive instruction as were the youngsters attending Worcester's only factory school at Webb's Carpet Manufactury – something like the local equivalent of a northern textile mill. In 1846 the building accommodated forty little factory girls – all volunteers, provided with their own schoolmaster and no rules except that 'they were clean' when they entered class.

Church and chapel were already deeply absorbed in the work of education. That increased even more with the expansion of Sunday schools and the Government's decision to fund and utilise religious day schools as the best way of educating the masses. So until the Forster Education Act of 1870 and the creation of state 'board schools' to fill the gaps, religious schools had virtually the monopoly of popular education.

The needs of Sunday scholars at the Worcester chapels were taken very seriously. J S Hanson, best known of the Baptist organisers, seemed to dedicate most of his daylight hours to organising a religious reference library for his part-time Sunday school teachers. The grand new Congregational chapel in Angel Place was extended in 1888 to include a splendidly large building for its Sunday scholars with no fewer than twenty-three classrooms built round the large central hall. A different kind of free church congregation met at The Countess of Huntingdon's Chapel in Birdport, a crowded area up from the river with poor housing. In 1878 this chapel boasted four Sunday schools with six hundred children and sixty teachers. In later years an additional class was developed for young men who met on a week-day evening for prayer meetings supplemented by earnest discussions on worthwhile topics like 'Abstinence' and 'Is it Right to go the Pantomime?'

Religious control over day schools had increased markedly. The departure point in 1809 was a local lecture by Joseph Lancaster, the pioneer of the so called monitorial system, when he outlined his 'new and mechanical system for the use of schools'. In other words training senior pupils to teach the others – which clearly an attractive method because of its directness and cheapness. The first Lancastrian or 'British school' was in St Martin's Gate in February 1811 with 352 boys on the books. Obviously a similar scheme was also feasible for the Anglican church. The National Schools were based on monitorial ideas devised by Andrew Bell and starting with St Peters in 1812, National 'parish' schools spread across the City. Once a venture began in the parish, the authority of the rector was paramount. The gothic styled building in Infirmary Walk, for instance, which was linked to the Church of St Nicholas benefited from the kindly but firm evangelical authority of Rev W H Havergal. His daughter, the poet and hymn writer, Frances Ridley Havergal, took a deep interest in the children and had them in mind no doubt whilst composing her poem *The Great Teacher*.

'He chides me not, but waits awhile,
Then wipes my heavy eyes;
Oh, what a Teacher is our God,
So patient and so wise'

National schools became associated with both old and new parishes in St Martin's, St Peter's, St George's, St Nicholas's, Holy Trinity, St Stephens and over the river in the parishes of St John's and St Clement's. At St Peter's the original building was adapted from an old riding school, and pupils from the school went on to become some of the most talented amongst the apprentices at Worcester Royal Porcelain Factory. Government cash helped to pay for staff salaries; the princely sum of £36 a year was set aside for a teacher at the first British School run by the Nonconformists. But no such a government grant would become available to the Catholics when they began their first day classes in four rooms behind the presbytery. Their expenses were met entirely from voluntary subscriptions. Instruction in this school benefited greatly from the exertions of The Daughters of the Heart of Mary, a teaching order especially recruited for their pioneer spirit. So successful were they, that the Rev I Bradshaw Tyrwhitt, the Anglican curate at St George's Barbourne, started up a school of his own in a disused cowshed, expressly with the purpose, of keeping local youngsters free from the snares of Catholicism.

But how good was the progress? The log book for St Paul's Church School fifty years later, indicates that problems had scarcely got easier with the passage of time. We note that the Three-R's were inculcated into children with steely persistence and that lessons were supplemented by fierce drilling in the school yard by a sergeant sent down from Norton Barracks to put the pupils through their paces. At this stage the school was receiving visits from a schools inspector, the shrewd and kindly Mr Spackman, who appeared keenly aware of the virulent epidemics raging through Worcester and drew urgent attention to the filthy outside toilet block in the infant school 'unclean and malodorous' he wrote 'they require daily attention from the caretaker'.

Many children were still not educated and the act of 1870 made it obligatory to offer school places for all children between five and eleven. The gap in Worcester's educational provision was met by new government board schools like the building constructed at Hounds Lane in Birdport – a locality of great poverty. 'Mitching' or truanting, was common. There was also an intriguing column on the school register for cryptic explanations. Here we find for the late 1890's brief comments where a pupil had left or quit suddenly. Ivy Hurley and Alice Taylor were removed 'due to mother's insolence'. And next to the names Nellie Bradley and certain others who departed before their time, we simply read the words – 'no reason given'.

## The Older Pupils

The inadequacy of Britain's secondary education had become the subject of fierce debate. It certainly amounted to more than a shortage of school places. There were arguments about fees, about classical bias in the curriculum and the neglect of science, and ignorance of business and commerce. In a nation which existed on industries and crafts, how and where would the young learn how to use their hands?

All these issues were fully played out in Worcester. Until 1867 the scholars of the King's School still desported themselves in mortar boards and were engaged in regular fights with their rivals 'the frogs' or boys from St Peter's Day School on the opposite side of the street. But when a person with as powerful an intellect as Canon Mandell Creighton wrote to the *Worcester Herald* in November 1889 about the curriculum and organisation in Worcester's secondary education, something was likely to be done.

Progress in both Worcester schools throughout the early 19th century had been somewhat patchy, despite a number of undeniably impressive academic entries to the ancient universities. Arguably the most gifted and unappreciated teacher at Kings was Thomas Baxter. The son of a brilliant porcelain painter, Baxter had no university degree and soldiered through his long teaching career 'hot tempered but kind', imparting to pupils a deep love of natural history and drawing. His meagre salary was supplemented by marginal extras like being the official supplier of text books and acting as school usher or disciplinarian. Those on the King's register of 1865 included a pupil with the splendid name of Homer Demosthenes Voltaire Kirk. His would be the rising generation for whom greater things were planned for influential voices began arguing it was time to aim for a single first rate educational institution in Worcester' properly endowed and funded But what was the plan to be?

Worcester's other historic foundation, Queen Elizabeth's, was still confined during the 1850's to its cramped building nestling against St Swithun's Church. It was one of the schools fiercely opposed by that bold and somewhat self-righteous radical, George Griffiths. As a campaigner Griffiths claimed that the ancient Midland grammar schools were being modernised completely the wrong way. His original charge against Queen Elizabeth's was inefficiency. One day he walked into the small old building to find the master absent and only three bemused pupils in attendance. But once Queen Elizabeth's had moved to more spacious surroundings in the Tything, they were freshly attacked for abandoning the terms of their founding charter and charging fees. Griffiths flatly refused to accept any argument that fees were necessary to pay for a more ambitious educational curriculum and imposing new buildings on a different site.

And so in the late 1880's a mighty argument over modernisation took place over which institution would take precedence - the Cathedral School or Queen Elizabeths? In the course of the battle it became obvious that both sides could muster influential supporters. One option was the amalgamation of both schools with King's offering facilities for those desiring a traditional classical education and university entrance. It was a proposal clearly offensive to Queen Elizabeth's now facing redesignation as the place for those aiming at professional and occupational careers – 'the commercial school of the town 'as it was condescendingly described .

Unsurprisingly the proposal came to nothing and was abandoned. The status quo triumphed, honour was satisfied with both schools moving onwards and upwards to secure their separate reputations.

For parents with money other forms of private tuition were always available. There had been an excellent 18th-century Quaker academy, and a number of local clerics were always prepared to take on pupils in order to supplement their stipends. The young Edward Elgar was placed in private Catholic schools firstly in Britannia Square and then at Littleton House, Lower Wick.

At Britannia House in the Tything a school was set up for the instruction of 'young gentlemen' run by Leycester Lynes, a flamboyant mystic who soon disappeared to become Father Ignatius, the first Anglican monk. In 1883 the same vacant building was carefully scrutinised for occupation by Worcester's first high school for girls. The venture was launched under the watchful eye of Canon Butler at the Cathedral with powerful backers like Earl Beauchamp and John Corbett who were persuaded the hour had come for girls to be privately educated. The first headmistress, Alice Ottley, was determined to set the loftiest Victorian standards. 'Our Lord Jesus Christ is the headmaster of this school' she proclaimed, and advised her girls never to read a novel before 12 o'clock in the morning. Drill classes were held under the instruction of a specially trained Swedish drill mistress with the girls singing together as they drilled, to the refrains of *Tit Willow and the British Grenadiers*. There were plenty of special occasions. In 1893 Lewis Carroll was present, entertaining 'the juniors' with his favourite mathematical puzzles, and in 1893 there was a classical music concert arranged by a Miss James and a Mr Edward Elgar.

In 1866 the empty Commandery building in Sidbury became the site for a significant innovation in special education. One of the housemasters at Kings, R H Blair had acquired a pupil who had been blind from birth, which was used as a reason for founding a Blind College for the Sons of Gentleman. As well as acting as the first principal, Blair had taken on the task of administering to one of the poorest city parishes. It was a disastrous overloading which broke his health. Fortunately this did not jeopardise the future of the college which benefited from the generous benefactions of Miss Eliza Warrington* and was rebuilt on a more substantial scale in Whittington Road.

* See A Short Biography of Eliza Warrington by Brian Ferris.

Vocational and trade education became an urgent priority as the Victorian economy was exposed to the chill winds of international competition. Like other industrial towns Worcester caught the mood of the 1851 Exhibition and established its own Government School of Design. It became an institution associated with the very brightest artistic talent. Amongst its best students were Tom Bates, the Rushton brothers, James Callowhill, the porcelain painter, Sir Thomas Brock, the sculptor, James Hadley, the modeller, B W Leader, the painter, and H Martyn, the wood carver. Writing in the local press R W Binns, General Manager at Worcester Royal, encouraged the public to give this educational venture their strongest support. 'Our work', he claimed 'is only just begun'. The depth of his own conviction to the cause was abundantly proved by the management policies at Worcester Royal Porcelain Factory and its apprentice school, famous for high artistic standards.

And not to be discounted was the School of Church Art and Embroidery run by Miss A M Parmitter where genteel young seamstresses learned to work on stoles, frontals and banners. 'Their catalogue' explained one reverend commentator, 'should be in the hands of every clergyman'.

In 1894 there was an important step forward. With considerable civic éclat and the presence of royalty, the Victoria Institute was opened as a centre for cultural and artistic encouragement. It had been conceived as an imaginative combination of art gallery, library, and art school located within a stately pile of terra cotta buildings. In other twentieth century cities like Exeter such bold experiments would eventually be transformed into universities. Alas in Worcester it has been deemed more appropriate to convert the building – or much of it into a block of flats. 'O tempora o mores!'

# Transport

One of the well known visitors was William Cobbett – bold, perceptive spokesman for just causes and a tireless traveller. Arriving in 1826, he pronounced Worcester 'One of the cleanest, neatest and handsomest towns I ever saw'. Indeed one of his only disappointments was over the scarcity of turnips grown locally in the countryside. Cobbett had come into town on horseback staying nearby at one of the many staging stops on his famous *Rural Rides* across England. It was a predictable way to travel but there were other methods of getting about even at that time. Transport was developing fast and 'communication' would become a theme to fire the imagination of Victorians.

Change and innovation, they believed would usher in a better age. In the past Worcester had always relied heavily on waterborne traffic and 'the goodly Severn' as John Evelyn once described it. This longest river thoroughfare in Britain was passed over by vessels laden with Shropshire iron, coal, and other Midland products with a multitude of goods coming up from Bristol in the other direction. The single most urgent priority was an improvement scheme for deepening the river channel. This would have prevented episodes like that occurring in the dry spell of June 1839 when 120 vessels were left grounded on the Severn shoals. Until 1842 any moves were blocked by powerful landowners with riverside rights. But in that year the bill passed through Parliament permitting the necessary action and the necessary fund raising. Soon the offending shoals at Diglis, Bevere, and Holt were dynamited, and large river locks constructed with weirs for the passage of fish.

With the coming of railways, modernisation was clearly the only way to compete. Worcester businessmen with a hint of desperation promoted ambitious projects to send vessels berthed on the Severn on longer seagoing voyages. Local entrepreneurs in the Severn Shipping Company, owners of the 146 ton, 'City of Worcester' in fact planned to make Worcester into a transhipping centre linking the Severn to an invigorated canal trade. Such hopes, alas, never materialised and though the 'butties' or boat people remained a lively part of the local community, big commercial interests now swung relentlessly over to the railways. The Worcester Birmingham Canal had opened in 1815 – taking twenty-five years to build. Factories and workshops grew up along the banks, but its fifty-eight locks and narrow width made it a difficult operation to run commercially and its fortunes suffered a bad blow when the biggest carrying company of them all, Pickfords, decided to transfer their canal warehouses over to the railways. In 1864 the canal company was unable to pay any shareholders' dividend. If not complete ruin, this was a serious blow, and afterwards the company became inclined to play things safe and steady. In later years there would be a slight boost in trade. The opening of Cadbury's model chocolate factory at Bourneville on the Worcestershire side of Birmingham was especially beneficial. Milk supplies were sent up the canal from a collecting point at Blackpole on Worcester's outskirts, and canal families earned a bit extra by bringing loads of hay up to Birmingham and then fetching back cargoes of Black Country coal for the return. Theirs was a distinct pattern of life and pubs like the Camp at Grimley specialised in providing the butties with their 'bait' and ale. Other waterborne traders were the wherry operators, ferrying in those folk with their produce from outlying villages – a smoother journey perhaps than using the carts and public wagons.

By Victoria's reign the fast mail coaches were offering quite an impressive service. Worcester was well placed on the strategic network, and there had been dramatic improvements in carriage design. New axles were designed to hold a whole month's supply of lubrication, and the new eliptical springs could withstand the jolting, and 'putten to' was the familiar expression for a speedy change-round of the horse teams - now perfected to a fine art. Expert coachmen, known as 'artists' proved time and again how they could cover routes at consistently high speeds. The road out through Great Witley with its regular milestones exemplified the pattern of reliable turnpike routes – a system which still prevailed in parts of Worcestershire until 1895. It was the maintenance of good road surfaces which allowed the coach, *Hibernia*, to make its celebrated run in 1832 from Liverpool to Worcester in 11 hours, 6 minutes. The City boasted seventeen fast coach services with associated hostelries able to provide respite and accommodation and always nearby an abundance of stables, fodder merchants, and farriers. In 1851 Worcester possessed some twenty-four local fly and gig owners with numerous suppliers of saddles and harness. Traffic chaos is not a new problem. The City Police Force established in 1833 struggled hard from the outset to impose some kind of order. All the carts and carriages, wains, and drays were supposed to be weighted, and their wheels should have been fitted with fellies or rims with countersunk bolts to save the street surface from damage. The Town Police Clauses Act of 1847 included a set of general regulations forbidding anyone driving more than one cart along the road at a time. Also shoeing, bleeding, or farrying a horse at the roadside was forbidden. Market days were horrendous when the narrow congested streets became a bedlam of grinding wheels. Parts of the City Centre became choked up with all the different carriages:– gigs, flies, wagonettes, growlers, and chaises. And for the more prestigious travellers, there were elegant phaetons and landaus – some of them craft built at the carriage works of McNaught's in the Tything.

The railway did not have a smooth arrival. Like certain other towns Worcester flirted with potential railway companies but came off badly. The first line was constructed by 'outsiders' and bypassed the City at Spetchley to go speeding onwards towards Cheltenham and Gloucester. Ironically the business meeting which dealt this blow to Worcester took place in the Star Hotel in High Street. Much blaming was to follow based on the reality that the local citizenry could only catch their train by struggling up to Spetchley Halt in a horse omnibus (the despised 'Spetchley Nuisance').

This was not the way of the future, and Worcester business interests were desperate to find some better arrangement despite major impediments like those neighbouring landowners who seemed ready to clamp down on any scheme whatever. But the strong voices including those of the new Chamber of Commerce were demanding not merely a new railway line but – specifically 'no railway but one which came right through Worcester'. Clearly they were seeking to reclaim somehow Worcester's favoured position on the old coaching network.

The spate of fresh negotiations produced a wide choice of schemes and considerable squabbling. At one stage thirteen different railway projects were lodged involving Worcester. The new broad gauge proposal was outlined at the Guildhall by Isambard Kingdom Brunel himself and hailed by its supporters as a truly revolutionary innovation. It was a bitter business with the vested interests behind each scheme obliged by law to carry on their protracted infighting both inside and outside Parliament as well as attempting to assemble some kind of funding package.

So only in 1850 did the first rail link to the south finally appear with a temporary station at Shrub Hill. The controlling company was the OWW – the Oxford Worcester and Wolverhampton, popularly nicknamed – 'the Old Worse and Worse'. And not for two years was the link further extended northwards as far as Stourbridge. The Oxford Worcester and Wolverhampton Railway directors and their backers in the GWR were playing for high stakes. They wanted to push north from Oxford but well beyond Worcester to exploit the fast growing wealth of the industrial territory embracing Kidderminster, Stourbridge, Wolverhampton, and Birmingham. If they faltered, the advantage would be seized by their deadly rivals the London and Birmingham Company linked to the Midland Railway. The complications became nightmarish. A decision about a railway line to Worcester was suddenly handed over by Parliament to a special committee of the Board of Trade which kept changing its opinion. The key question of whether or not to adopt Brunel's broad gauge was passed to quite a different group of commissioners and got caught up in a lofty argument about free trade. With vested interests using their leverage inside and outside Parliament and serious additional uncertainty over funding, the result was partial completion and interminable delay.

Afterwards railway fortunes began to improve. In 1861 a connection to Hereford and beyond was opened, bringing in cheap Welsh coal over the high viaduct and iron river bridge to the great advantage of Worcester households and businesses. Further developments were to follow. Shrub Hill Station was improved and expanded to create an additional main platform for the Bromyard Leominster line. A steep siding was constructed to peel off at the Butts in order to transport horses to the racecourse. Another single track veered off between two engine sheds to serve the Hill Evans Vinegar Works crossing a main road but with a speed limit of only four miles an hour.

Shrub Hill was now the centre of a triangular railway complex of railway sheds – reputedly including the main carriage works of the Great Western Railway. Unfortunately a big fire in 1864 caused the GWR to change their plan and relocate carriage building to Swindon. There still remained ambitious prospects for railway engineering in Worcester. The *Illustrated Midland News* of November 6th 1869 contained a glowing account of the Worcester Engine Works. The economic collapse of this enterprise was only just round the corner but the article gives no hint of impending financial crisis. The emphasis was on bold technical ambitions and the fine lay-out of this industrial site. The works was described as 'a handsome substantial building'– offering employment for up to a thousand men. Notable production achievements were proudly recalled including the fixed engine for Worcester's Waterworks Company, forty engines for The Great Eastern together with, 'a large number of those magnificent engines which run upon the Metropolitan Railway' and 'a large order for Russia'. But none of this business nor the girders ordered for the Usk Viaduct and those for Smithfield New Market prevented the final collapse.

A longer running success story was enjoyed by the nearby manufacturing site of Mckenzie and Holland. Their principal output was a brand of railway signalling which became renowned throughout Britain and its Victorian Empire. The essence of the business was interlocking signals, an ingenious system preventing points on the track being used independently of signals. Mackenzie and Holland originally used a clever but complicated arrangement of cams. The superior 'Deakin' method utilised a simpler tappet or sword iron to engage with a series of cross members. When the Deakin Patent lapsed, Mackenzie and Holland swiftly seized their chance and introduced their own locking frame incorporating the tappet method, together with inventions by the firm's own talented engineer, F W Coomber.

73

Such innovations had a major impact on railway travel. The 'pointsman' on duty no longer needed to be hyperactive and the chances of railway disasters was greatly diminished. Local people would not need convincing for they would recall the notorious accident of 1868 when eleven schoolchildren were killed on an excursion train returning home to Wolverhampton from Worcester. So we can see that despite a late start, railways had become an integral part of Worcester life. Theatrical companies like D'Oyly Carte travelling up to perform at the Theatre Royal arrived by train, with all their scenic props and masses of luggage. And the Worcestershire Naturalist Club embarking on their Jubilee Excursion were able to command the use of the Great Western Railway's directors' special saloon viewing carriage. In the Club's annual transactions the Honorary Secretary expressed his warmest appreciation. How often, he mused at the start of their field meetings 'had they all assembled at Foregate Street and Shrub Hill'. Their history could not be written 'without tribute to The Great Western Railway'.

Local newspapers in 1888 proudly advertised that all principal trains were met by tram. The tramcars in their livery of cream and Brunswick green crossed the city, charging a flat rate of a penny for any distance. And two year's after Victoria's death, they were electrified in a major extension of Worcester's generating capacity. Their steel lines were not such good news for the safety of cyclists. Owners of two wheeled machines as well as tricycles and velocipedes were increasingly numerous. In any case the police took a dim view of cyclists. They were altogether too active, vigorous, and unregulated. It was absolutely illegal for them to trespass onto the footpath. It was further decreed that cyclists must always dismount speedily on the roadway should any horse, mule or other beast of burden become 'restive alarmed or out of control'. Finally in July 1896 came the printed notices from the Chief Constable warning all cyclists 'against furious riding'. By the death of Queen Victoria, every kind of transportation seemed to be in a state of hyperactivity. Traffic in the city centre was becoming dense enough to cause serious jams, and it was to stop things grinding to a halt that they decided to fetch down a whole section of the High Street for street widening.

Constant and hectic changes were taking place in all aspects of transport, so had people forgotten how to walk? On the contrary, they walked great distances, even to seek work. In 1808, William Billingsley, the Worcester floral artist of true genius, tramped all the way from Swansea with his two small daughters, just to find employment. Brushmakers and tin plate workers were amongst those who frequently marched from town to town, stopping off at the Plough where the landlord ran an unofficial employment agency. Our Victorian ancestors were prepared to walk miles merely to satisfy their curiosity. A public execution or a big case at the assizes could bring in the crowds from miles away. Imagine the scene at the Lent Assizes in 1845 when they rolled in from Pershore in droves. Eleven poachers appeared before the Lord Chief Baron Pollock charged with the murder of Lord Coventry's gamekeeper in the course of a desperate affray between keepers and poachers at the gate of Park Farm, Pirton. Every exciting ingredient was present. Had the nobleman's keepers provoked this battle with bludgeons themselves? How reliable was the witness George Lippett who had turned Queen's evidence, or the full confession of Francis Dingley who was trying to save his neck? As they listened excitedly in the public gallery, those who had tramped the long march from Pershore might consider the effort was worthwhile. Their walk had earned them a hearing at one of the classic Game Law trials in British legal history.

# Politics

## Early Politics

If Victorian towns were noisy a great deal of the turbulence arose from arguments over politics. That was certainly true in Worcestershire. Public contests throughout the County had always been robust affairs. We remember how in 18th-century Kidderminster, voting in a new bailiff was traditionally accompanied by an aggressive ritual of pelting with cabbage stalks, and at Evesham an essential part of the mayor making ceremony was to ply the candidate with drink and then throw him off a gardener's cart. True the passage of time caused some of these extravagant practices to disappear, but elections never quite lost their wild unpredictable character.

In Worcester the City's historic status had earned it the right to send two MP's who until the constitutional changes of 1885 were returned along with ten other members from the surrounding county. Throughout the 19th century parliamentary reform would remain the dominant issue with its supporters relentlessly forceful in their expectations. Before Victoria came to the throne, the Reform Act of 1832 increased the Worcester constituency voters though there were still only 2940 on the electoral register. The way people actually voted was crude if not perilous. Until the passing of the Secret Ballot Act in 1872, polling took place in full public view with individuals going up to cast their choice in the hustings fully exposed to the hurly-burly of the crowd. Under the old system the voting went on endlessly. In the year 1818 the election was to continue for a space of seven days in a classic example of boisterous politics.

One of the successful candidates Col T H H Davies, a stalwart of Waterloo and a political outsider, was obliged to spend £12,000 on the election itself (a fairly modest contribution compared with earlier times) and then another £8000 on fighting an electoral petition through the courts to prove that he had not fiddled the result.

Two of the elections before Victoria's accession – May 1831 and December 1832 – were dominated by this passionate campaign for a large measure of parliamentary reform. As in so many Midland towns the political atmosphere became highly charged when reform campaigners attempted to break the hold of the old regime at Westminster and its local stalwarts at the Guildhall. Violence broke out on the streets arising from several causes. There was anger against Bishop Carr living in the Old Palace for his opposition to the passage of a reform bill in the House of Lords at a key stage. The crowd was obviously stirred by events further down river at Bristol where the Bishop's Palace had been set on fire. The Mayor, Henry Clifton, did nothing to conceal his anti-reformist sentiments, ostentatiously swearing in large numbers of special constables to keep public order. After a day full of disturbances the Yeomanry Hussars swept into the City just after the Mayor was struck by a brick whilst reading the Riot Act. Events as forceful as these remained deep in the Worcester consciousness for years to come. Politics might have seemed quieter but the big issues remained uppermost. Throughout 1836 and 1837 people still crowded into noisy Guildhall meetings convened for the purpose of petitioning parliament to introduce the secret ballot. Highly vocal opinions were expressed at these gathering, too risky and too uncongenial for the local press whose reporters dwelt on the fears of those opposed to reform and all it stood for – 'Treachery and hypocrisy' – a corruption of public morals'. The leading political traditionalist and noted horticulturalist, John Williams of Pitmaston House, St Johns, actually surrounded his residence with high walls to withstand the onslaughts from the populace which he now anticipated. Party politics in the ensuing years lacked clear definition but there was no lack of strongly expressed views. Certain activists now demanded that much more be done for the poor and excluded sections of the community. 'Discussion on socialism is rife in Worcester' claimed T C Turberville in 1839, the year when Robert Owen, a father figure of that movement, appeared at the Guildhall to debate with his ferocious critic, Dr Brindley, the Stourbridge schoolmaster. The local press, highly critical of Owen and all he stood for, reported that the meeting had to be abandoned just short of a roughhouse and 'in the utmost confusion'. In fact similar tumults took place at other Midland towns which makes it more than likely that local industrialists had sent along a group of their tough workers deliberately to stir up trouble.

By the late 1830's those most motivated for action and change were the Chartists. Their belief was in a fully accountable Parliament with voting rights for all men as a prime article of faith – only then through genuine democracy would life get better for everyone. Their principal leader, Feargus O'Connor was demonised by the authorities but seemed highly popular amongst many industrial workers like the Kidderminster carpet weavers and the Worcester glovers. O'Connor liked Worcestershire, choosing it for the sites of some of his experimental land colonies in the so called Chartist Land Plan. Worcester workers took part in the lottery draw where the prizes were cottages with associated parcels of land in the settlements of Great Dodford, Snigs End, and Lowbands – not then part of Gloucestershire.

During the 1842 slump, Chartist sympathisers turned out in large numbers to a big Guildhall meeting which had been called to discuss the economic crisis in the City. 'Every street, lane and alley' reported the Berrows News 'sent forth its crowds of distressed and dissatisfied poor'. It was obvious that the Mayor, Edward Evans, would be completely unable to control proceedings despite his urgent pleas for disciplined debate. Here was an audience out for blood: first came a frontal attack on the Corn Laws – 'Upheld by public swindlers and thieves' claimed one speaker. Anger then erupted as someone appeared to forward the solution that the poor be asked to emigrate. A voice from the floor shouted that, – 'If emigration was supposed to be the answer – the first emigration ship might be filled with dukes and lords' (loud cheers!) By this time, the Mayor had already quit the chair in disgust at which point the proceedings were hijacked by Chartist supporters. By the time they left the building, a resolution adopting the six points of The Peoples Charter had been moved and accepted. The local press reacted with shock and disbelief. This outcome, they implied could only be due to the influence of outsiders from Birmingham!

By the beginning of Victoria's reign Worcester's choice of MP's were no longer scions of the local aristocracy. One prominent outsider who got selected was Sir Thomas Wilde, the Attorney General, famous for being a defence lawyer in the case of Queen Caroline, the estranged wife of George IV. In later elections the choice increasingly fell upon significant representatives from the local business community.

The astute solicitor, William Laslett, who first stood in 1852 had come up through the Liberal ranks on the Council and was an benefactor of Worcester's first public cemetery. Laslett was an early critic of the Corn Laws and their dire effect on food prices which was a stout platform for winning urban votes. Once a sitting MP he could make a laudable stand on matters of principle. The Palmerstone government's grab at Chinese territory, he condemned as 'most unchristianlike' and also advocated graduated tax increases on the rich, the abolition of capital punishment, and a wide extension of the right to vote. But sensing a big change in the political climate, Laslett opportunistically shifted his allegiance and stood for the other side. He attempted to portray himself very much his own man as Laslett 'the renegade rad' (i.e. radical) and played up to the religious vote as a 'Protestant of the very first water'. But unfortunately he still lost the election.

Three other Worcester industrialists elected to Parliament were Richard Padmore, the ironmaster, A C Sheriff, a railway baron, and Alderman Hill, proprietor of the large vinegar works. Laslett later decided to transfer his political allegiance to the Tories and lost. All the others flew their flag with the Liberals who for the moment had become the dominant political force. Liberals as in other towns traded on the memory of Tory mismanagement under the old system. They attracted many professional and businessmen into their ranks, kept a keen eye on the rates, and appealed strongly to the Nonconformist vote – by no means a trifling consideration in elections both local or general.

The major change of 1835 to a fully elected council brought some strong personalities to the Guildhall – stout hearted tribunes of the people who were anxious to pursue local issues. Two of Worcester's prominent medical men seemed particularly blessed with a social conscience.Henry Hebb, a distinguished physician and heart specialist, turned his ordered mind to investigating abuses in the running of many of the city's historic charities. Charles Hastings, founder of the body later to become the British

Medical Association, was decidedly one of the new breed: a doughty campaigner for the abolition of slavery and an enthusiast for parliamentary reform. His activities during the terrible cholera outbreaks made him the natural leader in Worcester's fight against dirt and disease. Here was a political battle difficult to win. The government might be prepared to nod in the right direction but the initiative must be seized by each individual municipality. Hastings and his allies, Lord Lyttleton and members of the so called 'clean party', mounted the political drive for a public health board – a discretionary body with powers to supply a proper water supply and a drainage and sewage system for Worcester. The opposition hit back with accusations of inordinate expense on the rates – a scheme investing dictatorial power in the wrong hands. Not until 1858 was an important part of the plan achieved as the Corporation finally gave permission for constructing a municipal water works at Barbourne involving unparalleled levels of expenditure by local standards.

Pride and even a degree of self-righteousness were much in vogue. Alderman Padmore and Alderman Rowley Hill were such firm Congregationalists that they refused on principle to wear a robe and process as usual for events in the Cathedral. Joseph Wood as the mayor in 1861 insisted in using his power as chief magistrate to restrict the opening times of pubs and shops on the Lord's Day. Our Victorian ancestors were more than capable of getting worked up about local environmental matters. In the 1860's, opinion was well fired up and began attacking the Corporation when they refused to pay the relatively modest cost for redeeming the bankruptcy of the company running the Arboretum private pleasure grounds – a green treasure which gave pleasure to many. Thirty years later it was Pitchcroft, Worcester's largest open space, which faced a similar peril. This time, fortunately, a solution was hammered out; the public became more vocal. It was a characteristically Worcester compromise. Full public access would be guaranteed if some of the costs were borne by Earl Beauchamp and if Pitchcroft could continue as a racecourse as well as the drilling fields of the Worcestershire Yeomanry.

## The Later Politics

The parliamentary vote was widened in 1867 but not without another reform act and a period of national anxiety. The unrest in London and Birmingham could easily have spread further, and the mood on the Worcester Watch Committee with responsibility for the police force and for law and order was distinctly edgy. The Committee sent to the Government urgently requesting that Worcester's police force be armed, but Her Majesty's Inspector of Constabulary, General Cartwright, responded bluntly. Armed police, he claimed were dangerous, – 'not being sufficiently trained'. It was hardly likely to relieve the tension of the Worcester authorities who probably thought about using other agencies like the local yeomanry to keep order. The records of the King's School at this time show their army cadet corps had certainly been practicing drilling, skirmishing and volley firing, fixing bayonets and training with heavy carbide rifles since 1864.

In party politics it looked as if better organisation was the real key to success. After another extension of the vote in 1884, the Liberals lost their overall political control, just at the time when the Worcester Constituency was reduced to a single member of parliament. Conservatives and Unionists as they became known were receiving powerful backing from big brewers, partly due to the Gladstone's government's drastic interference into liquor licensing. The Clarion, Worcester's short-lived new style magazine summed the situation up nicely. 'Beer has a bigger pull than vinegar', they wrote on the defeat of Alderman Hill the Liberal Candidate – pressing home the point that he was principal partner in Britain's largest vinegar works. The Conservatives appealed to patriotism at a time it was running strongest, and they seemed able to call on the services of highly influential people even where they resided outside the City boundary. Sir Richard Temple, the retired Governor General of Bengal and MP for South Worcestershire was a capable administrator with an assured touch and interestingly modern views including a belief in votes for women.

Worcester also had a number of sympathetic theatrical operators. William Gomershal, charismatic manager of the Theatre Royal, showed the way to drum up popular ardour for the Boer War, and Walter de Freece from the Alhambra Music Hall went on to be a Tory MP with a title as well as the husband of Vesta Tilley. There was no doubt that the Conservatives operated an effective political machine which they proved once again in the parliamentary election of 1895. On that occasion the Liberals only fielded a candidate right at the last minute. Their man was speedily branded in the local press as an interloper, 'Mr Hincks of Leicester. Mr Hincks certainly had a fight on his hands. The most influential local newspaper was in the ownership of his political opponents, and many of the pubs under the management of their supporters. Worse still lots of football sides had been receiving their competitive trophies and prizes from the same source – especially due to the football sponsorship of local pubs.

Neither did Liberals choose their main election issue terribly wisely. It was to be Home Rule for Ireland, though Mr Hincks did have more hope with his policy calling for fairer housing leases from landlords. In the end, the so called Radical Liberal Hincks produced quite a respectable result – polling 2320 to an Alsopp vote of 3530.

This occasion and the general hullabaloo of Worcester party politics drew public attention away from mounting allegations about serious corruption in Worcester elections. The public up to that point seemed comfortable with the notion that the newly reformed parliamentary system had done away with most of the old voting irregularities. True, there was obviously cause for unease in the 1868 election when a cartoon caricatured Laslett as a horse in Worcester Races called 'Conscience Money'. But as time progressed the accusations became more serious, especially once the Liberals began losing their elections after 1886 and looking out for reasons. Widespread rumours began to spread about large scale election bribery leading to the fiddling of votes. The questions were finally answered only after Queen Victoria's death when evidence was published showing voting shenanigans going back over several decades. To prove matters it was decided to hold a special parliamentary commission for investigating 'extensive bribery at Worcester'. The full facts when published revealed a great deal more about Worcester and the conduct of elections since the 1860's, with particularly close investigation into the way voters had been bribed through 'treating' in any number of pubs and social clubs.

Reading the detailed statements of witnesses we get an absorbing account of what exactly went on during those busy election days. The whole election business was highly managed and Worcester generally was whipped up into a carnival atmosphere. Party rosettes were distributed by the bagful and horse drays bedecked with party ribbons sent up the side streets to winkle out every available voter (in party organisers' parlance called 'working the backs'). One of most fascinating witnesses was a certain Mr Martin of St John's Ward. 'Why had he accepted his 'treat' of a monetary bribe'? asked the cross-examining prosecuting barrister. Mr Martin answered back with marvellously Dickensian aplomb –

'I always had half a crown a Parliamentary' he replied, 'and I shall not go without it'.

The final years of Victoria's reign were politically active and not least in 1900 when local Conservatives received quite a nasty shock to the system. Returning home after his term as Governor General to New South Wales, Lord Beauchamp of Madresfield became a sudden convert to radical liberalism. During the next reign he would prove himself as a Liberal spokesman on a range of matters from workmen's compensation to Ireland. Whilst on the local political scene, the Liberals gained greatly from all his wealth and social influence.

Within Worcester the Liberals had also been improving their operations at the political grass roots. 'Dickie' Fairbairn, the young tramways manager, had proved himself a highly successful city councillor and astute election organizer with a talent for hard-hitting campaigns on vital issues. He attacked the city's inadequate housing stock and the exclusion of certain poverty stricken individuals families from hospital treatment at the Royal Infirmary.

Willis Bund the brilliant but crusty Chairman of Worcestershire Quarter Sessions always held the jaundiced view that little good ever came out of Birmingham. But for many it was difficult to resist the political appeal of Birmingham's famous 'civic gospel' – the view that any great city should be mindful of the welfare of all its citizens. The doctrine certainly made an impact in Worcester once the city had been granted full powers as a county borough, despite its relatively modest population figures. Amongst the influential businessmen sitting as councillors, there were undoubted converts to Jo Chamberlain's Birmingham 'Unauthorised Programme' for municipal reform. A full blown manifesto was ruled out on grounds of expense but Worcester council members saw an advantage in promoting certain civic projects (like the electricity generating station and serving breakfasts to the poorest children at Hounds Lane Board School) as long as costs had been carefully scrutinised and there was the chance of winning over some working class votes. That approach also had the endorsement of an influential opinion-former like Canon Mandell Creighton of the Cathedral Chapter. He would have preferred Worcester and Worcestershire councils to go even further and take a firm grip on their educational powers. 'They like to talk about it (education) but they do not wish much to be done,' he claimed in his speech to the Worcestershire Union of Workmen's Clubs and Institutes. According to Creighton most British men now had the vote, and so a decent education was crucial. 'Men must learn to think for themselves' if democracy was to succeed.

Those not well off still had far to go. In October 1872 forty branches from the surrounding agricultural districts sent numerous delegates to a conference of the newly formed National Agricultural Labourer's Union in Silver Street followed by a meeting at the Guildhall in order to discuss basic pay and conditions in the countryside. The Worcester Coop too was proving a highly purposeful movement, well beyond its status as a popular retailer. Its saving schemes, social clubs, community education, and financial support for embattled trade unionists made it a foundation for radical action. For local trade unionists the times had become harshly confrontational. In 1894 the local ASRS (Railwaymen) were locked in a fierce but unsuccessful dispute aimed at moving Worcester pay rates up to parity with those of Midland Railway workers from other districts. An equally fractious dispute involved the sizeable number of local men employed in engineering who had joined up to the ASE (Amalgamated Society of Engineers). In previous years this body had been very much a craftsman's organisation – almost an elite. Older members would remember that they were once obliged to serve a full seven year engineering apprenticeship. But having 'served their time' they were rarely short of work and invariably regarded as highly respectable and studiously moderate in their dealings with management. The 1890's changed that when the union made the fateful decision to open its ranks to a wider group of machinists and semi-skilled workers The management at the Vulcan Works in Worcester and other engineering employers were ready to take a tough line. The argument was over basic working practices: shiftwork, piecework, and overtime. Management had equipped their workshops with a new generation of expensive machine tools:– automatic lathes, planing machines, and drills. To operate profitably, they now needed a preponderantly semi-skilled workforce prepared to work the new machinery round the clock. It was a world away from the old days of the Worcester engineering craftsmen and their time-honoured practices.

The long bout of bad labour relations with much political embroilment really began after 1888. That year the Worcester branch reported to their executive in London that the unpopular production practice of piecework was virtually unknown in local factories. But three years later it was a different story. In that short space of time piecework had become 'a great evil to the working man'. Management was absolutely insistent upon its use, imposing a lock out which hit local factories in 1897. It was either piecework or no job in Worcester engineering.

Worst still the Amalgamated Society of Engineers Union could not even get the going pay rate for their craftsmen employed by the council on two projects at the Water Works and the Worcester Electricity Works. But hard times brought resilience too and a revived interest in politics together with an awareness of other workers and their struggles in distant places. The union branch voted levies from their meagre funds for some of the highest profile disputes of the era. In 1888 they paid towards the famous London Dock Strike. In 1890 it was for railwaymen in Scotland and in 1891 for the linen lappers of Belfast. In 1897 they aided the carpenters of Brussels and in 1901 the Danish engineering workers. Was there some vested interest here, some ulterior motive? Probably not; just a beleaguered local union branch showing it possessed the vision of a wider world.

HENRY CLIFTON     MAYOR 1831

III

V

VI

VII

# List of Coloured Ilustrations

Cover Pictures.
Steamboat passing the cathedral from a letterhead of the 1860's

Vase illustrated by Callowhill and Bott
(by kind permission of the Worcester Porcelain Museum)

Photograph of Shirehall Statue

Back Cover (detail). Bought in Worcester?
County ladies portrayed in their finery at a yeomanry review
(by kind permission of the Worcestershire Yeomanry Trustees)

I. Worcester's rural setting painted on a plate,
probably by George Stimson Snr.
(by kind permission of the Worcester Porcelain Museum)

II. Mayor Clifton, enemy of reform

III. Mayor Lewis, friend of commerce

IV(a). Worcestershire Sauce celebrated in porcelain
(by kind permission of the Worcester Porcelain Museum)

IV(b). From a postcard of Hill and Evans

V(a). Work of apprentices at Royal Worcester
(by kind permission of the Worcester Porcelain Museum)

(Vb). Porcelain floral painting by Worcester artist, David Bates
(by kind permission of Worcester Porcelain Museum)

VI. Ornamental gates at the Victoria Institute
(photograph by Barbara Burton)

VII. Floral illustration by David Bates.
(by kind permission of Worcester Porcelain Museum)

VIII. From a postcard of Spreckley's Brewery

# Religion

On a dark December day in 1870, the diarist, Francis Kilvert, arrived for the funeral of his Aunt Maria. She had resided in the privileged recesses of College Green and was to be accorded the prestigious burial suitable for those within the charmed circle. Kilvert records the solemn procession across The Green to the booming of the great bell. Then, an almost disastrous near collision happened between the coffin and the Cloister Arch due to the venerable pallbearers and their lack of stamina. 'The Psalm was sung nicely to a very beautiful chant' and 'Canon Wood read the lesson well and impressively in a sonorous voice'. The diarist departed for home on December 3rd, evidently impressed with Cathedral life – even more so in the knowledge that his aunt had not left her entire fortune and effects to the Chapter and Diocese.

Kilvert also noted that there had been great changes. After 1844 the number of canons in the Chapter was substantially reduced – their stipends used for the benefit of poor parishes. The structural fabric especially had long been a cause of great concern. So much so that in 1833, Rickman, official surveyor of the fabric, actually warned the public about entering the building to attend 'the music meeting' as the Three Choirs Festival was then termed. The only answer appeared to be a major restoration. When completed it seemed more like a transformation. The work lasted for years and years involving several architects, endless committee meetings, and all manner of subcontractors and associated craftsmen.

It was decided not merely to rely on the services of Edward Perkins, the resident architect, but to bring in the expertise of more illustrious colleagues, notably Sir George Gilbert Scott. Control of the project was deemed too significant to be left to ecclesiastics alone, and much of it passed into the hands of prominent County laymen. An especially prominent role was assumed by the Earl of Dudley – generous both with his money and his opinions. Big arguments arose over a series of important issues with Sir Gilbert Scott finding himself forced onto the defensive. There was controversy over renovation of the famous tower, over the screen, the cloisters, the organ, and most of all the nave and choir.

Over the nave and choir Lord Dudley had strong ideas (especially if they were to be restored with the benefit of his cash). Both in his view existed for the purpose of divine service, and decidedly not for concerts. This meant a clear prejudice against The Three Choirs Festival dismissed as performances 'by English and foreign artists – of indifferent reputation, greedy of pay, then as now and barely able to pronounce the language, they were paid to sing in'.

It was suggested the best answer was to move the festival out altogether so the newly restored nave could be permanently 'fitted for divine service' – 'for the hundreds and hundreds of people living in the city'. We can now look back on the incident as a curiously Victorian wrangle, but at the time it caused a minor furore.

The general health of The Church of England had long been a cause for concern. Archdeacon Warren of Worcester had warned his clergy as early as 1763 against 'lukewarmness and unconcernedness' in their religious life. Two of the specific problems were pluralism and absenteeism as demonstrated in the career of a Dean of Worcester, George Murray, who for many years before 1841 was also Bishop of Rochester. For the best example of cloying deference often accorded to figures of authority, we have to turn to Mrs Henry Wood. In her story *The Channings* there is an incident where the Bishop of Hestonleigh (the fictional Worcester) is accidentally locked up in the cloisters through the carelessness of an aged Cathedral retainer:– 'a pretty situation'- The Right Reverend Bishop of Hestonleigh ranking about fifth, counting by precedence, on the Episcopal bench, locked up ignominiously in the cloisters of Hestonleigh with Ketch the porter and Jenkins 'the stewards clerk'. The like had never been heard of.'

As time passed much was done to improve such matters. Exemplifying a new approach Mandel Creighton, who was appointed a canon in 1885 threw himself vigorously into the life of the whole community –using his influence for instance to create a pleasant cathedral garden overlooking the Severn and challenging local political leaders to look for genuine rather than token advances in popular education. The more robust approach to Christian morality can be detected in the writings of Worcester's most celebrated authoresses. As well as Mrs Henry Wood there was Mrs Martha Sherwood who published the final part of her Fairchild Family saga in 1847 – one of its less appealing purposes being to inculcate a sense of guilt in the very young.

The influence of religion overall remained strong. Over the centuries Worcester had become a hive of occupations associated with the church. Ebeneezer Bayliss, printers and publishers of Bibles, maintained a Worcester tradition going back to John Oswyn, one of the earliest English printers. The organ builder, John Nicholson, had been drawn away from building textile machinery in his native Rochdale to workshops near St Alban's

Church which produced the finest church organs in the business. Jones and Rowe, the boiler makers, took a special pride in their 'Witley Court' boiler for heating draughty churches. Worcester's workers in stained glass were George Rogers who made windows for Gloucester and Worcester cathedrals and the designer F W Preedy who also doubled as a busy church architect. Most eminent of the local sculptors was Sir Thomas Brock, one of whose countless effigies of Queen Victoria, presides over the Shire Hall forecourt. Worcester's most successful sculptural firm belonged to the Forsyth brothers and operated from their workshops in the Tything. The most accomplished wood carver was John Martyn who beautified the Cathedral's Jesus Chapel and added to the decorative grandeur of Mount Battenhall.

Worcester was also a well known centre for those in search of church lace and priestly vestments, as well as being the location of a highly genteel school of ecclesiastical embroidery. Even the Hill Evans Vinegar works worked to something of a religious agenda offering as their secondary line of operation, the production of British fruit wines, which could be happily consumed by those who had taken the pledge against strong drink.

The later Victorian period was the time when the Church of England paid much greater attention to its poorer parishes and to Worcester's burgeoning suburbs. With different options in 'churchmanship' on offer, worshippers at St Nicholas could enjoy their low church evangelicalism with hymns and religious tracts by Frances Ridley who was a daughter of the parish incumbent.

Old St Martin's with its Frederick Preedy stained glass was destined to become a haven of the Oxford Movement perhaps a somewhat risky tendency in a diocese where in 1881 one priest was convicted 'of Ritualism' under the Public Worship Regulation Act of 1874 and spent a short term in Warwick Jail.

Wherever there was a substantial area of new housing, a new church would usually materialise. For St Pauls in the Blockhouse, A E Street's polychrome brick church was constructed. And for the railway workers suburb along the Astwood Road, they built an economical brick church by the local architect Arthur Day, dedicated to St Barnabas. Within the new Holy Trinity Church opened near Shrub Hill Station in 1865 it was found possible to incorporate the reconstructed roof of the ancient Cathedral Guesten Hall. It thus avoided the fate of six other important Worcester monastic buildings pulled down in the years between 1840 and 1860.

At every turn everyday life in the City illustrated the power of religion. Elgar's brother-in-law confessed in his diary the desire to visit 'every church and chapel in Worcester'. But he could still bemoan what he described as the ravings of certain local followers of Sankey and Moody. In his opinion they ought to be locked up.

But there were some telling expressions of sincere and simple faith. For instance the 1898 minutes of the Amalgamated Society of Engineers, a leading craft union, include a letter of condolence from 'Brother Thomas', the branch secretary to a member whose wife had died –'We say cheer up, brother for we know as men, we look only at the present and sometimes dark side but with God things are different.'

The local Catholic congregation had deep Worcestershire roots nourished with the blood of martyrs. But they still battled against fierce prejudice including angry meetings at the Guildhall called by those who opposed the creation of new Catholic dioceses in England. Despite this, Catholic fortunes in Worcester had markedly improved. Hubert Leicester, Elgar's lifelong friend, wrote about the heady enthusiasm with which the congregation beautified their church in Sansome Walk, a building which was embellished by a fine copy of Raphael's *Transfiguration*. In 1851 the church drew on a congregation of 480 and was already known for its music before the young Elgar started composing for its services in 1876. The City's Catholic mission was fortified by the active community of nuns which had moved into Stanbrook Abbey. There was also the patronage of the Hornyolds, affluent county landowners who married into Italian aristocracy and were thereby elevated to a papal dukedom. And not the least of the blessings was the devoted service of Fr. William Waterworth who was widely respected for his learning and christian example.

Protestant denominations were also prospering after many years of persecution. The Quakers had their meeting house off Sansome Walk and the Baptists had settled into to their strikingly gothic premises in Sansome Walk. The Congregationalists in Angel Place derived from the flock assembled – in 1687 by that 'faithful and profitable preacher of the Gospel', Thomas Badland. For thirty years the minister was Dr George Redford, a substantial theologian and a natural leader whose efforts in the words of one local supporter 'were highly blessed'. Members of the chapel's community were powerful figures in the City so much so that Congregationalists became something of an alternative establishment class. Their wealth and influence resulted in the construction of fine new building with a semicircular portico of Corinthian columns jutting out confidently into the street, its large glass dome illuminated by 364 gas jets. On each side of the portico were separate entrances to the galleries, one specially for the boys of the Sunday school, the other side for the girls, so that 'no noise or unseemly collision will be allowed to disturb the congregation'. The main Wesleyan Methodist Chapel in Pump Street boasted large evening attendances of 425 with lively branches springing up in St Johns and Barbourne. The Primitive Methodists established themselves amongst the poor residents of the Blockhouse as early as 1824 not far away from Zion Chapel in Park Street run by The Wesleyan Methodist Association. Almost midway between them in Carden Street lay the building familiarly known as The Hall of Science, seemingly a place of worship on Sunday for Chartist sympathisers but used on weekdays for dancing. By 1851 the worshiping here was done by the Worcester branch of The Latter Day Saints with 50 members and a certain number of others who were described as 'adherents'.

There was yet more. In the course of Victoria's reign Worcester produced Secularists and at St Nicholas Street the body of Christians who would acknowledge 'no Sectarian Name' – advertising their meeting place as 'The Room'. The Salvation Army came to town in 1881 making rapid progress after acquiring The Old Alhambra Music Hall for their headquarters in Lowesmoor. Theirs was the message of 'conversion on the drum', taking to heart William Booth's precept that the odds were four to one in Satan's favour. Their war against ungodliness was waged in the streets and in the pubs with the magistrates normally siding with the Salvationists against the rowdies who threatened them. But there was a famous occasion when the Law went the other way and the Salvationist Captain Osborne was packed off to prison for preaching without a license. His short time behind bars in Worcester however did not prove a comfortable experience for the authorities. Each Sunday the assembled ranks of brothers and sisters paraded round the walls of Worcester Jail with their resounding refrain 'We are marching, praying and singing for you'.

One of Worcester's most singular congregations was located in a delightful classical chapel in Birdport built in 1809 – with its outstations in some of the surrounding villages. The Lady Huntingdon Connexion included earnest followers of the doctrines of John Whitfield and Calvinistic Methodism. The Worcester chapel prided themselves on their special loyalty to the traditions of the founder, Selina, Countess of Huntingdon which involved scrupulously careful liturgical observation. In 1862 for instance the Reverend T Todd, the minister, wore a surplice for communion but for preaching always a black Geneva gown.

The Connexion's principal work was in the central district of poor households up from the river. The exertion of much buoyant evangelical energy produced worthy respectable citizens like Moses Thomas who became Mayor and a leading member of the City Council. The Connexion also became known for its zeal in overseas missions especially to Sierra Leone in West Africa. The cash raised from all those chapel bazaars and Sunday collections was not sent to conventional white missionaries but directly to the black Christians or 'our coloured friends' for their 'united and extensive efforts'. As early as 1851 one of the black missionaries arrived in Worcester hoping to raise even greater help. 'Our sable friend' as he was called, preached about his missionary work at the Birdport Chapel and all the village outstations. But we also find him at the Guildhall speaking impressively about the horrors of slavery still existing in West Africa. Here was practical Christianity in earnest.

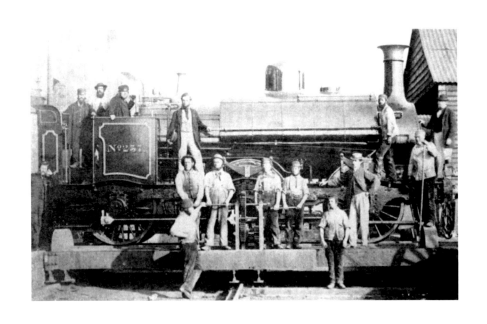

XIII

XIV

XV

XVI

## FANCY DRESS AND SILK WAREHOUSE.
### (Established upwards of Half-a-Century.)

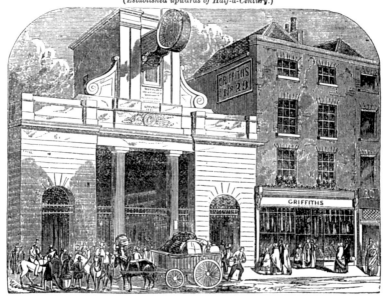

XVII

XVIII

XIX

XXII

# List of Black & White Illustrations

# Some Victorian Specialities

# Worcestershire Sauce

Lea and Perrins did not make their fortune by false modesty. From early days they claimed their product as the connoisseurs' choice 'THE only good choice'– a condiment so 'unrivalled' that many unprincipled dealers might be disposed to purloin its trading name for their own 'spurious compounds'. Such a degree of self-confidence took the firm a long way, and when that didn't work they resorted to the law courts. Their biggest victory was in 1906 when a legal judgement by Mr Justice Swinfen Eady decided that whilst others could employ the name 'Worcestershire Sauce' only that of Lea and Perrins could boast to be original and genuine.

Underlying it there needed to be a clever commercial strategy, for in Victorian times light piquant sauces of the type were common, and Worcester itself was the home city for at least two rivals – Mellors and Courtneys. The owners of the latter firm ceased trading when the going got tough and went into the scrap metal trade. Lea and Perrins on the other hand always thought out their operation much more carefully. They had started as owners of a group of enterprising chemist shops. The first was established in Broad Street, Worcester in 1823, then at Kidderminster, Malvern, and Cheltenham offering such exotic sounding potents as Dover's Powders, Tartar Emetic, Turkey Rhubarb and Ipecacuanha Wine – in the sound traditions of Worcester's well known 18th-century apothecaries. There was always an eye to the possibilities of overseas trade. Trusses were shipped out to miners involved in the Californian Gold Rush as well as an interesting line in fancy cosmetics like luxury soaps and a concoction for gentlemen's hair described as Marrow Pomade. Sauce making became a serious line of business in 1837 – the year of Victoria's accession. At first it was made in 4 gallon jars and then in casks of 28 gallons using only the most healthy of ingredients which would be kind to delicate constitutions: malt and spirit vinegar, molasses, sugar, salt, anchovies, tamarinds, shallots, garlic, spices, and other flavourings.

An important part of the game was keeping the recipe and the whole production process secret, almost mysteriously so. Bottle labels from the 1840's described exactly how the original formula was discovered. It was 'from the recipe of a nobleman of the County' who brought it into the chemist's to have it made up. Highly imaginative rather than accurate, this was to become a famous marketing legend.* The noble personality in question was thought to be Marcus, Lord Sandys but he did not come into the title until 1861. However impossible, the story was cultivated as an excellent piece of publicity as the sauce was advertised and distributed all over the world. An important task was choosing the best agents and giving them sufficient discretion. Powerful wholesalers like Crosse and Blackwell were selected, and in 1853 the agency in the USA, John Duncan and Sons, organised the award of a prestigious medal for the sauce at the New York Exhibition, and in 1899 production for the US market was handled from New York to avoid the heavy new import duty. A clever piece of advertising was to publish compliments and anecdotes from all over the globe. One of the best, probably gleaned from Army Public Relations was taken from a letter sent by a soldier in The South Wales Borderers after the battle of Rorke's Drift in 1879. 'We managed to get potatoes now and then and occasionally a bottle of Worcestershire Sauce without which you could not distinguish the ration beef from leather.'

*See also chapter six.

The Firm's sharp instincts even caused them to pay attention to the size and shape of the bottles and particularly to the style of the labels. These were printed with the care and attention normally reserved for bank notes. By 1900 to avoid imitation or falsification the red and black wrapper was overprinted with a prominent signature in white bearing the firm's name as a 'distinctive feature for the guidance and protection of the Public'. This was a company which was directed locally and by 1900 was into its third generation of family ownership; having provided Worcester with three mayors. John Wheeley Lea, one of the founding partners, typifies that sense of municipal earnestness found amongst many of his fellow businessmen. Involved in establishing the local chamber of trade, he was also a generous contributor to the Royal Infirmary and in 1840 held the appointment of its Inspector of Drugs. At the end of the century control of the firm passed to Charles Williams Dyson Perrins, a highly able business leader and prominent local benefactor. Dyson Perrins finally drove through the long-delayed move from an outdated city centre premises to a purpose built factory in Midland Road near the railway line. Already involved in banking, his refined aesthetic taste made it a natural move for him to extend his business interests into Worcester Royal Porcelain where in 1898 he organised the first of several financial loans destined to save the firm from extinction as well as rescuing its priceless museum collection of antique porcelain for posterity.

# Porcelain

It had arrived in Worcester rather suddenly in 1751 with all the attributes of a glamorous and fashionable industry. But porcelain manufacture was always an uncertain trade and without several changes in company ownership and a constant stream of new ideas, the factory would quickly have gone out of business like so many of its competitors.

Such problems did not disappear in the 19th century, and in 1840 it was necessary to merge the Company with the Chamberlain Porcelain Manufactory in a so- called 'marriage of convenience'. The organisation did not assume its new title of Worcester Royal Company until 1862. And in later years there would be further amalgamations. In 1889 Grainger's, an important local rival, was taken over and in 1905 the business established by the ceramic modeller James Hadley was absorbed after his untimely death. The consummate skill of Worcester's craftsmen might prove more than a match for any rival, but the overall trading position continued highly difficult. Output now concentrated at the Diglis works had to be constantly varied and intensified to steer the business clear of receivership and permit a modest expansion in the labour force. After their somewhat disappointing showing at the Great Exhibition of 1851, the firm made great efforts to enhance their reputation. A new series of strikingly designed set pieces were a bold attempt to restore prestige. The Shakespearian Service of 1852 was based on the theme of a Midsummer Nights Dream, modelled by W B Kirk and painted principally by Thomas Bott. In 1865 Worcester produced its ravishing jewelled tea service for the Countess Dudley with the panels exquisitely painted by Thomas Callowhill. Ceramic figures were now produced in large quantities to become a staple part of the factory's output.

Worcester's craftsmen and craftswomen too were often locals, highly talented and trained on site and at the Government School of Design in Pierpoint Street. The apprentices taken on at fourteen were carefully instructed in botany, anatomy, and the rudiments of ornament often turning to old master paintings for further inspiration. The Victorian factory became renowned for a number of its artistic names: – painters like Thomas Bott, the Callowhill brothers, Luke Wells, David Bates, and Charles Baldwyn. Its inspired modellers included – W B Kirk, James Hadley, and George Owen whose speciality was pierced ware or porcelain perforated by a thousand holes each executed by hand. Much of this fine porcelain was gilded – a skill in its own right as demonstrated in the career of the foreman – Samuel Ranford foreman gilder over many years. The driving force was R W Binns, Managing Director and Art Director. Under his guidance the Worcester factory derived much that was best from the prevailing designs and from those of the past. Binns was a good businessman who brought in new unglamorous commercial lines to help square the books. They included vitrified stone china for hotels, shipping lines, and railway tea rooms. Under his management an industrial laboratory came into use, and he introduced gas to fire the kilns as a more controlled and economical form of fuel. The Company was now exhibiting its wares internationally at Chicago and Paris, and visitors came to the factory in their droves enticed by advertisements from the *Penny Magazine* and other popular journals. Binns was responsible for building up an historical collection of Worcester ware – a world famous museum* archive as an aid to design and an inspiration for the future. This Worcester factory did not represent the sum total of china manufacturing locally. At St Martin's Gate there was the smaller works of Graingers whose 'semi porcelain' or chemical porcelain earned its own reputation. Another firm, Lockes, catered for a different market – for collectors of heraldic or crested souvenirs.

James Hadley produced what he termed faience. Early in his life Hadley was Modelling Master at the Government School of Art and lived to become one of the most brilliant ceramic modellers of the age. His premature death was a tragic blow to Worcester. But as we know too well today, the porcelain trade was never a stranger to misfortune.

*This world famous museum is still a major visitor attraction.*

# Worcester Shopping

Shopping was an intense pre-occupation even in Victorian times. Late on Saturday night, short of cash, they descended on the Shambles in droves as the butchers without the benefit of refrigeration, sold off their meat. At the basic level was the small grocer. Slater's Directory of 1850 lists 124 of them in Worcester and its surrounding villages. What would they have been like? Maria Glover's shop was described as being in 'Blockhouse Fields', one of the poor areas, and it must have been similar to that corner establishment so graphically described by Robert Roberts in his famous study of early Edwardian Salford. It would have probably been looked after by the mother in addition to her other duties. It was open all hours from 7 am to an hour before midnight; a place to call in for a chat, where you could spend farthings as well as shillings. At such a Worcester shop in 1900, eggs would have cost you eight old pence a dozen – many of the other prices down on what they would have been in 1870. An order would often include cigarettes first brought into popularity by soldiers in the Crimean War. After 1883 cigarettes were either made by special machines or rolled out of tobacco taken from a tin box which had more than likely been knocked up at Williamsons Providence Works in the Blockhouse area.

By the old Queen's death part of the grocery trade had moved upmarket. Better off customers expected to be 'served'; first placing an order then deciding if they wanted it sent round by the shop boy. The national diet was improving largely due to a new style of grocery retailers like Liptons, the Maypole, and Home and Colonial. This type of shop was well represented in Worcester. The stores relied heavily on imported foodstuffs and achieving a high turnover with strictly cash sales and abundant advertising. People fed better – with more meat certainly though the choice was restricted – a bit of bacon, butter or margarine, not much in the way of fresh milk and eggs and above all the increasing consumption of tea – 'a prime comfort of life'. Another late Victorian innovation was eating fish and chips – a custom which had spread down from the north in the eighteen eighties. Worcester had its own special ice manufacturer on the outskirts of St Johns for keeping fish fresh. By the middle of the 20th century, Worcestershire boasted no fewer than two hundred and fourteen fish fryers – many in Worcester itself.

For those after a bargain the markets were always a popular haunt. There was an indoor market hall opposite the Guildhall dating from 1804 which had been extended and given an imposing side entrance into Pump Street. At least since 1867 the Corporation had been badgered to provide a proper site for a street market, instead of the chaos on busy days when South Quay was jammed solid with sellers wagons and carts. By the 1880's the Worcester Coop was also doing sterling work by selling food of high quality with a 'divi' and well organised savings scheme thrown in for good measure.

Worcester had long enjoyed a reputation for upmarket and specialist retailers indeed members of the Chamber of Commerce would have been be keen to point to those glorious 18th-century days when Worcester outranked York for its stylish shopping. Victorian commerce therefore possessed excellent foundations for all kinds of businesses:– tailors, pharmacists, specialist grocers, stationers and booksellers, emporia for fabrics and fancy goods. The columns of local newspapers were filled with advertisements from these traditional shops. In 1872 Messrs Twinberrow, chemists of Broad Street drew readers attention to the merits of their powders and liquids sold in either small quantities or in bulk. In common with Worcester's other chemists this firm maintained the proud traditions of Worcester apothecaries stretching way back into history.

If you were searching for travel goods in 1851 you would be drawn to the firm of I and J Moses – specialists in portmanteaus, trunks and what they described as 'railway wrappers' no doubt to keep out the draughts of the open carriages on the notorious Oxford Worcester and Wolverhampton line. For stationery goods it paid to visit John Stanley, of Sidbury who offered customers a wide choice of visiting cards 'In a very superior style'. Pratley's, the specialists in china were already well established when they moved in 1880 to their new shop in the Shambles. Alternatively fanciers of fine china could patronise the sales outlets at the Worcester Porcelain Factory itself, which had been organising visitor tours since the mid eighteenth century.

The prototype departmental store of William Whitely had opened in London in 1863, but even before this time provincial Worcester had its own rival establishment – Woodward and Woolrich. In 1855 at their High Street premises this firm offered the services of silk mercers, shawlmen, furriers, and hosiers and, also sold mourning and fancy bonnets with an immense choice of stays. It was also possible to order funerals from these premises 'for the peer or the peasant'. Around the corner at 3 and 4 St Swithin they had their other store – the household merchandising department offering: – mattresses, feather and flock, horse hair, wool with straw palliasses and Kidderminster carpets.

Customer choice was not lessened by the passing of the years for this was the City with a shop for almost every need. In the age before factory made clothing, drapery stores were particularly in demand. Simes and Turleys held in stock a wide range of fabrics and every variety of pins, needles, buttons, and buckles. They also sold corsets, underclothes, nightwear, gloves, and stockings. It was definitely a firm poised to become the departmental store of the future as was true of Russel and Dorrell which began their trading early as military tailors and suppliers of new surplices to the Cathedral. Quite a number of ladies wishing their garments to be specially made up gave their patronage to Rutter and Jones, a business happy to declare pride in their 'efficient staff of experienced dress and mantle hands'. As for ladies hats, in 1868 Worcester claimed no less than five millinery warehouses. Female beauty preparations would be less available. Cosmetics then were intended to improve upon nature, not to adorn. Chemists might sell lip salve with a touch of carmine for chapped skin, but face powder and rouge were for daring actresses like Sarah Bernhardt. They had to be smuggled in from Bond Street and the West End of London.

Gentleman's apparel was most studiously catered for by Armstrongs in Sansome Walk and at the establishment run by J Whitehead, a firm which advertised itself as having withstood 'the competition of the cheap ready-made clothing merchant'. For goldsmiths and watch and clock suppliers like Peplows, Worcester was renown. One watch firm eventually expanded into the firm of Kay's, the national innovators of the mail order catalogue. An indicator of prosperity was the number of photographic studios, with Worcester scoring highly. At the turn of the century Bennetts in the Tything proudly reminded the public that they had been taking 'likenesses' for over forty years. Their expertise, they claimed, had kept fully abreast of modern scientific development so that they were now able to execute the very finest photographic portraits ranging from vignette miniatures to full length presentments 'of some civic magnate'. More intimate photographic likenesses of children and animals were on offer at the premises of F C Earle. Perhaps only in its supply of taxidermists did Worcester appear deficient. Of the four operating in Worcestershire in 1896, Worcester alas, could claim but one. Only for stuffed animals was it necessary to go into Birmingham.

AMEN CORNER

# Elgar, the Victorian

Elgar left behind his own fascinating glimpses of a Victorian boyhood. He recalls ambling over to school in Lower Wick with his friend Hubert Leicester. 'Nothing escaped our notice – everything was adjudicated upon' – 'Our walk was always to the brightly-lit west.' He remembers having to keep two pence for the Cathedral Ferry reached through the Water Gate. Behind its great door someone had incised a figure of a salmon onto the old wall (which remains there to this day). And all across Payne's Meadows, claimed Elgar – 'the unthrift sun shot vital gold'.

In 1859 the family had returned from the tranquillity of Broadheath Common to reside in the heart of Worcester and the stimulus and sadness of urban life. In the space of two years Elgar lost one brother Harry from scarlet fever fever and then Jo aged 7 nicknamed 'the Beethoven of the family' from tuberculosis. His father's connections were to prove a great advantage. William Elgar kept a well known music shop and was organist, if not an especially passionate believer, at St George's Catholic Church. He was a visitor at the homes of many influential families as their favoured piano tuner. The young Edward Elgar was to become acutely conscious of this association with 'trade'. But if that held him back and denied him many chances, it also implanted a strong sense of Victorian purpose. Edward Elgar was much more than a sensitive romantic with musical talent.

At sixteen he was still trapped behind the counter of the family music shop in the High Street, deeply engrossed in his musical self tuition but was already getting known as a teacher of violin from which he could earn something of a living whilst busy composing. The move out of the family home to lodge at his sister Polly's gave him a greater sense of independence. He then moved again to the house of his other sister – Lucy and her husband Charles Pipe 4 Field Terrace, a quiet location with views of the Malverns – an address where he could begin composing in earnest.

It was after he married and left Worcester that Elgar achieved real fame. But he had already penned some of his most evocative compositions – *the Wand of Youth Suites, Sevillana* as well as his *Salut d'Amour* written in 1888 as an engagement present to Alice Roberts, the new inspirational force in his life. If Worcester was no longer his home its impressions had permeated deeply and would never be forgotten. 'I am still at heart the dreamy child who used to be found in the reeds by Severn side.' Another occasion was the day when as a twelve year old, he rushed home after being present at an inspiring orchestral rehearsal of 'the Three Choirs' –possibly the moment when he truly began working at the violin.

Within a few years Elgar had become a force on the Worcestershire music scene. He was conductor of the Ladies Orchestral Club, the organiser of music at the College of the Blind, and full time organist at St George's Catholic Church. In later life he found his period of service as conductor of music at Powick Lunatic Asylum could be turned to advantage. When encountering someone of more than usual pomposity he was known to interject 'When I was in the lunatic asylum---'

Elgar would carry away with him a store of Worcestershire memories and many friendships. He drew heavily on his mother's love of nature and of literature as well as her influence as a devout Catholic. There was also his profound debt to his wide circle of early friends, including Ivor Atkins, the future cathedral organist. And perhaps there were also dreams of a Worcester sweetheart, Helen Weaver – who inspired three polkas.

Was the patriotism of 'Land of Hope and Glory' formed during these Victorian years? If so it was deep but never narrowly jingoistic. His desire, as he often explained, was to write something 'that my fellow Englishmen might take to themselves and love'.

# Benjamin Leader Williams

Benjamin Leader was the artist of the rural idyl. His landscapes were more than true to nature, they were imbued with a vision of the idealised countryside. He caught the mood of the times. As the scars of industry spread across Britain, the public yearned for an art which uplifted the spirits by capturing that rural calm and beauty which was far from the 'maddening crowd'.

Born with the name Benjamin Leader Williams, he astutely retitled himself to avoid being saddled with a surname as common as 'Williams'. He became a student of the City's School of Design in Pierpoint Street also favoured by many talented employees of the Porcelain Factory; many of them like David Bates similarly inspired by the beauty of nature. Throughout his long career Leader seemed to possess the measure of things. He always had ambition and the personal drive to achieve success.

It was impossible to boast a more authentic local pedigree. Leader had actually been born in one wing of the Guildhall, when it was temporarily a private dwelling (not as once believed in Diglis House). His father was Chief Engineer to the Severn Navigation Commission then at an active stage of its development.

Benjamin was originally intended for engineering like one of his brothers who contributed so much to the construction of that great Victorian enterprise - The Manchester Ship Canal. But Benjamin was more inclined to follow his father's favourite hobby that of sketching and painting the scenes to be found along the banks of the Severn. After time at the Worcester Royal Grammar School and the Worcester School of Design, he entered The Royal Academy of Art School and was permitted to display his work there when still a student. Leader pursued his artistic calling with immense energy. He exhibited 141 times at the Royal Academy, and his art was always popular and pre-eminently saleable. The critics were not always kind. He was initially faulted for his attention to detail, as being over precise. His later work showed looser handling and was more impressionistic without losing its faithfulness to nature. Like his more famous contemporary, Millais, he often favoured the darker palette and the wintry landscape.

At his best he, Leader, was a romantic painter of real stature, cleverly capturing that soft light to be found in Britain's Western regions. His choice of scene ranged widely but he always retained his love of the Worcestershire which he painted time and time again – most evocatively, its expansive watery stretches of the Severn and its lonely inland hamlets in the fading light.

One of his paintings gained a special public favour – 'February Fill Dyke' Its fame was hugely enhanced when Theodore Chauvel's etched it as a print. It thus became arguably one of the best loved of all Victorian landscapes and a centrepiece amongst the fine collections on display at Birmingham's new Civic Art Gallery. So dearly was it admired by the public – they would not permit any alternative canvas to occupy that very special place on the wall.

# Busier Days at the Guildhall–

## The widening Influence of Worcester's Late Victorian City Council

When he died in 1877 Richard Wolff, the town clerk, was accorded a splendid 'sgraffito' memorial in the Cathedral though it was his successor, Samuel Southall, who came to wield the real influence. The records of Worcester Corporation for these later Victorian years reveal the Guildhall's much closer involvement in local life. Paying for it through extra rates and increasing public expenditure, however, was a different matter and the enthusiasm decidedly less obvious.

Most of the Corporation's traditional duties remained and so the pay roll still included a number of historic posts. The Mayor's Officer, in former days the policing supremo, was paid £15 a quarter with an additional £5 for being Inspector of Weights and Measures. The Bellman was Worcester's version of town crier and performed the task of publicising through the streets 'all matters not of an objectionable nature' for which he was paid a shilling every time.

Financial accounts reveal an intensification of many council activities. They show increasing amounts of money spent on functions like street cleaning and the laying of pavements where incidentally large numbers of heavy horses were deployed. In fact there is repeatedly a whiff of the stables about certain items of expenditure. We find a local dealer, J Barnett, receiving £128 in one quarter for horse fodder also a substantial amount to the veterinary surgeon. To F J Hall there is payment for horse medicines and to W S Carless for shoeing the Corporation's horses.

Much greater amounts were now required for funding both policing and health. Looking at the detail we note that there were charges on the revenue for the cost of maintaining and washing prisoners in jail and the upkeep of juvenile offenders at reformatory establishments. In 1902 for instance there were thirty-seven youngsters at so called 'industrial schools' including the training ship Formidable which was permanently anchored off Portishead. The Council also met the cost of conveying certain people to hospital and certain patients were entitled to the provision of meat, bread, and milk during their stay.

# Public Health

Public health was now a serious responsibility. Numbered amongst the officers of the City Council was a public analyst, Horace Swete, who at monthly intervals pronounced on the quality of the local tap water. For April 1889 he found it perfectly acceptable and drinkable though his analytical report contains alarming remarks about the colour:– 'deep amber with sediment and turbid and milky with Kaolin'.

The water works at Barbourne constructed years ago had done little to allay public criticism. There were loud complaints both about the sufficiency of the water supply as well as its impurity. Although in council debates these were dismissed as 'sentimental', one of the Corporation's main advisors, G H Ogston was forced to admit that Worcester water contained worrying amounts of animal pollution as proved by the presence of Albumenoid Ammonia – which existed at twice the level contained in the Thames supply to London. Put frankly the Council could no longer dodge the risk to health. They had little choice but to install a more effective filtering system for Worcester's water and at the same time search for additional sources of supply to satisfy increasing demand and the needs of an expanding population.

The Corporation's obligations as an 'Urban Sanitary Authority and Burial Board' went even further. In 1892 there was serious concern about the return of cholera particularly from Russian leather skins destined for the local glove industry and imported through the heavily infected port of Hamburg. Government ministries had also started to adopt a more hectoring tone on health matters, and there were stiff penalties if their regulations were not heeded.

It seemed as if miles of new sewers were being laid right across Worcester but even that was not enough. A top government official, Colonel Ducat, decreed that the City simply did not have the sufficient installations for the disposal of its sewage. Councillors and officials would be required to find out even more about modern civil engineering and what it had to offer including: flushing tanks and special ventilation shafts for dispersing the dangerous build up of sewer gas.

In the end a sewage works was finally constructed off Bromwich Road upon land bought from Earl Beauchamp and not on the more cost effective site originally identified at Diglis. That was apparently because local residents along Bath Road raised many objections about the possible stink. The Council gave in on that occasion but generally its voice of authority was being heard more frequently. It appointed a Petroleum and Explosives Inspector for enforcing new government safety regulations and installed a further inspector in the Guildhall back yard for the obligatory testing of Worcester's many gas meters. Gas supply was proving an important issue, and in 1889 the local gas company was warned that their recent hike in gas prices was decidedly unwelcome. Gas consumption had increased at an alarming rate – sixty million cubic feet in the last thirteen years and local people depended upon it heavily.

# Policing

Another fact of life was the growing power of the police. The resignation of the Chief Constable in 1890 on health grounds whilst under official investigation was cleverly staged managed to cause the minimum fuss. But the underlying trend was completely one way. In a big change, summons and warrants of the Court were no longer issued by the Mayor's Officer in his role as High Constable. After the Police Act of 1890 they were now served by the Chief Constable. And even if the extent of crime had not increased, members of the Council's Watch Committee appeared determined to do more about low level offences like the street betting which was rife amongst 'under 18' youths.

A serious fraud which never came before the courts was what we might describe as the case of the 'City Council Manure'. A sixteen page report compiled in 1890 records how massive piles of dung from the Cattle Market and Council stables had been sold time after time without keeping any proper accounts. Mismanagement went back years with the sum of £8200 having gone adrift of which £7380 was finally recovered. The successful ferreting investigation by the Council owed a great deal to the sharp accounting work of Hubert Leicester, the great friend of Elgar. In the end the Council brought a charge of gross negligence against four minor officials who were publicly shamed and censured.

# Council Control of Education

A more elevated Council preoccupation was schooling for the city's children. Hounds Lane was the largest of the new category of board school, built by government edict under the provisions of The 1870 Education Act. This was an establishment financed mainly from the rates and managed by an elected school board, operating from the Guildhall. Within its spacious and draughty gothic spaces some of the poorest children in the City were rigorously drilled in the Three Rs within the context of a limited curriculum. In 1903 the council published a thirty years assessment of the work of the Worcester School Board which gave fascinating insights into the early story of Hounds Lane. School inspector, F T Spackman, from the Guildhall appears to have provided firm but sympathetic and kindly guidance. He certainly would not have shared the opinion of that local 'big wig', John Willis-Bund, that teachers were 'whining mendicants'. At Hounds Lane extra curricular activities and treats were organised for desperately poor pupils, and the huge problem of 'mitching' or truanting was confronted full on. In 1885 a terrible winter accompanied by the ravages of economic slump brought even greater hardship to certain parts of Worcester. The school board dealt with the problem by arranging cooked meals for many children. A small property adjacent to Hounds Lane School was requisitioned as a special kitchen, and for the next twelve years the local kids were regularly able to tuck into breakfasts or nourishing meals of Irish stew followed by jam roly poly.

The Worcester Council was also involved in pushing for a more effective system of secondary education. Local business had joined in the national concern about the alleged inadequacy of the secondary school curriculum and the possible link with a sagging economy. So much so that in 1889 the Chamber of Commerce decided to back a resolution in the council chamber calling for the amalgamation of Worcester's two endowed foundations: the Cathedral School and the Royal Grammar. It proved a sensitive topic, the modernisers argued that both schools were too small to be effective but they had stirred up fierce partisan loyalties and the project was doomed to failure. What would now become the educational focus for change? The council decided to revive the earlier scheme for an educational institute which had first been mooted in 1884. Driven on by an energetic Library and Museum Committee, the concept of a multi-purpose building for library, museum, artistic, and technical education looked highly attractive. Matching finance was somehow levered out of so called Enfranchisement Funds as well as rents from Council properties in Bridge Street. The remainder was raised by public subscription for a Victoria Institute to mark the Queen's Jubilee. Here was one of those times when Worcester was on the move!

# Naturalists Antiquarians & Americans

Sir Charles Hastings commented that science gave no rewards to idlers. It was a charge that could hardly be levelled against nineteenth century environmentalists in Worcester. When the new building of the Worcestershire Natural History Society opened in 1835, it contained a library and lecture theatre as well as the large collection of exhibits. The first honorary curator was the redoubtable Edwin Lees who also served on the major committees for Zoology, Botany, Geology and Meteorology. The Society enjoyed the active patronage of Sir Charles Hastings as well as counting on the support of influential people like Lord Lyttleton. But the charmed circle would not permit women members until much later. The ban even applied to Charlotte Perrott, a remarkable female enthusiast who had moved into town from Fladbury where she had completed a project on wild birds. Her research must have impressed the worthies because they stretched the rules to accord her the privileged status of 'talented Honorary Corresponding Member'.

Amongst the other full members was Dr Harvey Holl, one time army doctor during the Crimean War, who was an expert on lichens and rocks as well as being joint proprietor of the Worcester Herald. Representing the Social Sciences was Jabez Allies, the folklorist, well known for writing about some fearsome elves, associated with various parts of the county. One of the newer members was the fierce but scholarly J W Bund, a Chancery Lawyer, who was an historian of considerable repute and was deeply involved in producing the Worcestershire volumes of the *Victoria County History*.

By the 1860's Edwin Lees had managed to mobilise another group of passionate environmentalists calling themselves The Worcestershire Naturalist Club. Under his leadership they went charging around the City and its rural hinterland searching for 'Sweet Ladies Tresses' and finding Lesser Periwinkles on Whittington Tump.

A gala occasion in the life of the Society occurred in 1895 with a celebration dinner at the Bell Hotel in Broad Street. The final course was composed entirely of unusual edible fungi:– Tricholoma Nudum, Clitocybe Nebularis or Cloudy Agaric, followed by Lactarius Deliciosus. Charles Pipe, one of Worcester's best known grocers, was truly delighted to be present but later worriedly confessed in his diary, that he had simply no idea what he was eating.

When the Worcestershire Archaeological Society commenced life in 1854 as the Diocesan Architectural Society, John Noake, an unusually energetic antiquarian was already voicing his disgust. Why were so many fine historic churches after years of neglect being 'mutilated' with patches of brick and rendering? At Cow Honeybourne Noake had found pig-sties against the church walls and a bread oven operating where the altar once stood. So understandably, the original aims of this new society were explicitly to promote 'the study of ecclesiastical architecture, antiquities and design...'

One special firecracker was ready to ignite. The ancient Guesten Hall had been allowed to fall into a ruinous condition and was to be pulled down. But *The Associated Societies Report of 1854* described it as 'the only building of its kind in England and perhaps the most beautiful hall of its size and date in Europe'. The Society joined the chorus of protest against this vandalism by the Cathedral Chapter and commissioned A E Street, a well known architect to make drawings which would facilitate an inexpensive restoration. But it was no avail; though the rapid demolition was followed by bitter denunciations. 'They have ruthlessly swept away a building which was altogether unique', thundered the Saturday Review. It must be said that the Cathedral Chapter learned their lesson and changed tack. Within a few years, they had all joined the society and were contributing positively towards a higher standard in ecclesiastical and public architecture. The new Albert Orphanage in St Johns, they decided to criticise as 'eccentric' gothic lacking 'simplicity and repose' and the new chapel at Astwood Cemetery was censured as expensive but of 'little delight'.

We wonder what sense they made of the architectural trends taking place in Worcester's sister in the USA ? In this second city of Massachussets skyscrapers were already appearing by 1897. It was a community where business 'called the shots' and where great stress was placed on large industrial buildings like The Royal Worcester Corset Company. That particular firm which proclaimed itself the biggest corset supplier in the whole world, so we may fairly assume that several of our own Worcestershire Victorians must have squeezed themselves into one of their products. But what impressed visitors were the buildings con-nected with education and culture. There was the Free Institute of Industrial Science, the Clark University, the striking Art Museum and the Antiquarian Society a veritable storehouse of important historical manuscripts.

Some form of mutual exchange with such a city might have done the 'the old Worcester' a power of good but despite a few attempts on the American side, nothing transpired. In 1846 Massachussets quakers successfully gained the support of their English brethren for a petition against a war over the disputed

Oregon Territory. In 1879 there came a warm brotherly gesture from the Cathedral Dean and Chapter who granted a request for a fragment of stone from the Lady Chapel to be incorporated into an episcopalian church. But it was difficult to imagine how such accord could proceed any further without a degree of special effort. In 1893 a real opportunity occurred when some benefactor presented a Worcester Black Pear Tree for planting in Elm Park – the American city's graceful stretch of open land The sapling was afforded a privileged location amongst a collection of the finest native barks and its inclusion was intended as a mark of affection – for the association 'with our English sister city'. Sadly there was no reciprocal move from the English side too many national pre-occupations no doubt or was it sheer indifference?

# The Battle of the Stained Glass Window

In 1851 a serious religious controversy was raging through the nation. The Pope had decided to establish a distinct and separate Roman Catholic diocesan structure – a decision castigated by the Prime Minister as an aggression 'upon our Protestantism' 'insolent and insidious'. It was unlikely a major cathedral city would remain out of the dispute, though nobody could have forecast how the installation of a mere stained glass window could become the focus of such bitter religious argument. The triple lancet window in question was to be sited in the Cathedral's south transept and dedicated to the late Queen Dowager who had once resided out at Great Witley. Firstly funds had to be raised from public subscription after which the artistic selection process began. The arrangements, suitably discreet and delicate, rested with a subscribers' committee under the firm chairmanship of Lord Lyttleton – the brother-in-law of Gladstone himself and reputed to be 'the centre of intellectual life and progress in the county'. Who, it was asked, would be commissioned as concept artist for so prestigious a project? Might the choice fall on Pugin, the outstanding propagandist of the gothic revival, or possibly Hardman? Both were rejected because of popular feeling against Catholics and the next likely candidate was deemed to be Arthur O'Connor. Lord Lyttleton had been asked to inquire as to what communion Mr O'Connor belonged – in other words was he a sound Protestant? The answer came that he himself was undoubtedly Anglican but that his father was Roman Catholic. For that reason alone, he was rejected for a commission which might have greatly boosted his artistic reputation.

Mutterings of deep recrimination began immediately. The editor of the *Worcester Guardian*, snidely attacking the selection body as 'The Worcester Gentlemen' queried if a bid from Raphael or Murillo would have been accepted, considering they too were Catholics. Poor O'Connor himself wrote to the paper that he had always been a member of 'the English Church' – in fact he had devoted his life to cultivating what he termed as 'a proper feeling' for its architecture and architectural accessories. He concluded that it looked to him like 'bigotry and oppression to deprive me'. The plot deepened when it emerged that at a packed town meeting, the claims of a solidly Protestant candidate had been pushed. The person finally selected, Frederick Preedy was thirty-one years old and belonged to a safely respectable local family. Both his father and cousin were the official government distributors of stamps. Frederick Preedy described himself as an architect having served time in the Worcester office of Harvey Eginton. For him the Adelaide Window was a major scoop. Up to 1852 the only real work he had obtained was a general renovation of Stretton Grandison Parish Church which could hardly be considered the cutting edge of architecture. As far as stained glass was concerned, his experience had been confined to drawing design cartoons for various windows produced by the stained glass maker, George Rogers.

The important new Cathedral window was again made by George Rogers. It portrayed the Tree of Jesse in the central light flanked by side windows with various saints included amongst whom was a figure of the estimable and lately departed Queen Adelaide. The work was finished off by an inscribed Latin eulogy composed by Lord Lyttleton, a prize winning classical scholar in his time.

But the arguments were not over yet. Complaints were raised that the colour effects were all wrong – far too blue. When light burst through the window – a uniform sheet of bluey purple spread across the Cathedral floor. It was a time when such views were taken very seriously. And the criticism could not be shrugged off since it came from no less a body than the Ecclesiologist Society – a highly influential group in the current spate of church restorations. There was also disapproval from William Butterfield – very much the ecclesiastical architecture heavyweight and an early colleague of Preedy at the architects' office.

Preedy's answer was immediately to put the blame on the glass stainer George Rogers. Had he not foreseen the problem when first shown a sample of the glass and pointed it out to Rogers? But nothing was done because Rogers claimed he was answerable to the committee not to the artist.

It had been an unfortunate, unilluminating affair. Preedy was obliged to learn how to make stained glass himself. Having done so, he both recovered and prospered, becoming amongst the most popular if drastic, of the Victorian church restorers. In later years the Adelaide window disappeared from sight behind the massive new Hope Jones Cathedral Organ. Was it literally a cover up, we wonder – hiding away an embarrassing episode?

# Exotic & Novel Interludes at the Museum

It was sometimes difficult to distinguish between the Foregate Street Natural History Room and the theatre especially in an age when science and archaeology were often expected to provide entertainment and a sense of wonderment. In 1840 when the British Archaeological Association met at Worcester, its keynote public lecture was widely advertised and accompanied by the unrolling of an Egyptian mummy. At a later event in 1850 the music was provided by a Rock Band using instruments literally shaped out of stone. Worcester's museum in fact was becoming familiar ground for exotic music and dance. A poster from May 31st 1847 advertises the guest appearance of an ensemble of female Ethiopian Seranaders: Cleopatra, Bona, Orynthia, Jonia, Imoida, Alethia and Vishna. They are commended for 'the originality of their performance, the modesty of their demeanour and the absence of all exaggeration in their pantomimic action'.

A later musical performance in the same year was by Mr Shapcot and his seven saxophonist sons. Its poster contained an elaborate mission statement from Mr Shapcot himself, explaining his convictions on the importance of cultivating musical talent and its bearing 'upon the Elevation of the Working Classes'.

There were also those happy occasions when The Natural History Room in the Foregate simply served as an overflow or substitute for the Theatre Royal. An early and memorable show respectfully invited 'nobility, gentry and public generally to enjoy a formidable theatrical extravaganza by the eleven year old Master B Grossmith, described as a 'Great Mono-dramatic actor'. The young performer began with a lengthy comic performance as Dick, The Miller then continued with a dramatic divertissement 'My Cousin Tom' in which he gave seven different impersonations including Bill Snatch, a bailiff and Sambo Quaco, a Negro in search of Law, Liberty and Love! In the third section Master Grossmith played Sir Silvertongue Santer and Lady Betty Brilliant and in conclusion the audience was offered a dramatic and operatic farcette with Master Grossmith appearing as Pickle Bob, a tiger and finally Sir Henry Bashful. At last the masterful youth had exhausted his repertoire.

# References

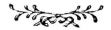

**Biography of Victorian Worcester**

Holyoake A V 1977 *Dear little Droitwich*. Bromsgrove: Market Place Press

The story of Greswolde Williams and the bear is told in this book. Unfortunately at Droitwich Station the bear broke loose from the packing case, escaped from the train, and was later shot in the grounds of Impney Farm.

**Links with the Past**

Cannadine D, 1990 *The Decline and Fall of the British Aristocracy*. New Haven, Con.: Yale University Press

Grundy M (ed), 1997 *Worcester at Work: Portrait of a Victorian City*. Worcester: Osborne Books

Gwilliam B, 1993 *Old Worcester: People and Places*. Bromsgrove, Halfshire Books

Jones L, 1970 *Customs and Folklore of Worcestershire*. London: Estragon.

Jones M M, 1980 *The Lookers Out of Worcestershire*. Worcester: Worcestershire Naturalists Club

Noake J, 1849 *Worcester in Olden Times*. London: Longmans

Report of Miss Bright's Wedding. *Worcester Herald*, Feb.24, 1844

Ryder V, 1989 *All Bull and Black Pears: a Celebration of One Hundred Years of Hereford and Worcester County Council*. Upton Upon Severn: Malvern Publications

Stafford T, 1837 *Guide and Directory to the City and Suburbs of Worcester*. Worcester T. Stafford

Tomkinson K, 1981 *Words of old Worcestershire*. Kidderminster: K Tomkinson Ltd

White F, 1962 *Good Things in England*. Edited by Florence White. Cookery Book Club

Worcester Cathedral Records See D1340 (i) and D1340 (xvi) Mr Day's Valuation of Houses Rentable

# Keeping Worcester Happy

## ~ A Survey of Victorian Entertainment

Davis R J, 1978 *Boating in Worcester in the Nineteenth Century*. Worcester: Russell Printers

Gordon C, 2000 *The Coventrys of Croome*. Chichester: Phillimore

Gordon H, article on *'Brothers of the Cricket Field'*. Windsor Magazine 1909 edition

L Q, 1914 *The Yeomanry Cavalry of Worcestershire 1794-1913*. Devizes: G Simpson (Privately published. Copy available at Worcester History Centre)

Maitland S, 1986 *Vesta Tilley*. London: Virago

McMenemey W H, 1947 *A History of the Worcester Royal Infirmary*. London: Press Alliances

Noake J, 1849 *Worcester in Olden Times*. London: Longman

Owen B R, 1992 *Worcester in Old Picture Postcards*. Zaltbommel: European Library

Pipe C, 2002 Diary of Charles Pipe. Article in *Worcester Evening News*, July 20, 2002 (all these diaries were published in this newspaper during the 1960's)

Smith L D, 1986 *Carpet Weavers and Carpet Masters*. Kidderminster: Kenneth Tomkinson

SudworthG 1984 *The Great Little Tilley*. Luton: Courtney Publications

Vockins M D, 1980 *Worcestershire County Cricket Club*: a Pictorial History. London: Severn House

Winspear S, 1996 Worcester's Lost Theatre. Hallow: Parkbarn.

## City of Work

Clarke A, 1988 *The History of the Net Fishermen of Worcester*. Privately printed.

Grundy M (ed), 1997 *Worcester at Work: Portrait of a Victorian City*. Worcester: Osborne Books

*Illustrated Midland News*, November 1869, Number 8 article on the Worcester Engine Works

Lyes D C, 1973 *The Leather Glove Industry of Worcester in the Nineteenth Century*. Manuscript. Published by the Worcester City Museum and Art Gallery in 1976

Newton R, 1968 *Victorian Exeter*. Leicester: Leicester University Press

Kilvert F, 1960 *Diary of Francis Kilvert*. Edited by W. Plomer. London: J Cape.

Webbs Chemical Manure Works Diglis, 1996 *Studies in Worcestershire Local History*

## Drink

Abbott E & Glover C, 1967 *A History of Worcester City Police 1833-1967*. Worcester: Worcester City Council

Clark G, 1849 *Report to the General Board of Health*. London: Clowes for HMSO

Dyson Perrins Worcester Porcelain Museum. Exhibition display

Green R, 1806 *A Brief History of Worcester*, 5th ed. Worcester: J Tymbs

Grundy M (ed), 1997 Worcester at Work: *Portrait of a Victorian City*. Worcester: Osborne Books

Gwilliam B, 1993 Old Worcester: People and Places. Bromsgrove: Halfshire

Hanson H, 1984 *The Canal Boatmen 1760-1914*. Stroud: Alan Sutton Publishing

Pipe C, 2002 *Diary of Charles Pipe*, Worcester Evening News, July 20, 2002 and in earlier extracts.

Winspear S, 1996 *Worcester's Lost Theatre*. Hallow: Parkbarn

## The Poor

Abbott E & Glover C, 1967 *A History of Worcester City Police 1833-1967* Worcester City Council

Aitken J (ed.), 2000 *Census of Religious Worship*, 1851: the Returns for Worcestershire. Worcester: Worcester Historical Society

Carpenter J H, 1972/3 *The Amalgamated Society of Engineers: the Study of a Victorian Trades Union, Worcester branch.*
Worcester: Amalgamated Society of Engineers

Clark G, 1849 *Report to the General Board of Health.*
London: Clowes for HMSO

Crompton F, 1997 *Workhouse Children.* Stroud: Alan Sutton Publishing
(I am grateful for the information in this article)

Grundy M, 2003 January 3: article in *Berrows Worcester Journal*
(I am grateful for the information in this article)

Hebb C, 1842 *An Account of all the Public Charities in the City of Worcester.*
Worcester: printed by Knight & Arrowsmith, Chronicle Office

Ittman K, 1995 *Work, Gender and Family in Victorian England.*
Washington Square, NY: New York University Press

Laws for the Regulation of a Provident Friendly Society of Married and Single Women. Instituted 26th May 1783 (Additional rule 1824)

Lee W E, 1992 *Mrs. Henry Wood in Worcester and Malvern.*
Published by First Paige

Lyes D, 1976 *The Leather Glove Industry of Worcester.* Worcester: Worcester Museum and Art Gallery

McMenemey W H, 1947 *A History of the Worcester Royal Infirmary.*
London: Press Alliances

Newton R, 1968 *Victorian Exeter.* Leicester: Leicester University Press

Ordnance Survey,1996 *Old Ordnance Survey Maps; Worcester Sheet 33.8 and 33.03.* Alan Godfrey Maps.
Facsimile reprint of map published by the Ordnance Survey, 1902

Pinto V (ed) 1965 A ballad started in 18c Worcester and continued at Shrewsbury and Coventry. published in *The Common Muse.*
Harmondsworth: Penguin

Saxton C, 1931 *The Origin and Progress of the Worcester Co-operative Society Limited 1881-1931.* Worcester: Worcester Cooperative Society

Smith L D, 1986 *Carpet Weavers and Carpet Masters.* Kidderminster: K Tomkinson

*Worcester Herald* November 1861

Worcester Parliamentary Election Petition, 1906 *Minutes of proceedings.*
London: Eyre & Spottiswood for HMSO

## Worcester's Well To Do

Abbott E & Glover, C, 1967 *A History of Worcester City Police* 1833-1967
Worcester City Council

Baldwin S, 1938 *The Service of our Lives*. London: Hodder and Stoughton

Gordon C, 2000 *The Coventrys of Croome*. Chichester: Phillimore

Gray R, 1997 *Witley Court, Hereford and Worcester*.
London: English Heritage

Grundy M (ed), 1997 *Worcester at Work*: Portrait of a Victorian City.
Worcester: Osborne Books

Gwilliam B, 1993 *Old Worcester: People and Places*.
Bromsgrove: Halfshire Books

Keogh, B, 1997 *The Secret Sauce: a History of Lea and Perrins*.
Worcester: Leaper Books

Knowles J M, 1995 *College Green Worcester, 1800-1900*. Worcester:
Worcester Cathedral Publications I am grateful for a number of references
from this most informative source.

*Littlebury's Worcester Directory for 1868*. Worcester: Littlebury

Sudeley Castle, Winchcombe item from the permanent *Victorian
exhibition display*

Williams D, 2001 *The Lygons of Madresfield Court*. Logaston,
Herefordshire: Logaston Press

## Building up Worcester

Attwood, D Unpublished research on housing

Barker, P, 1994 A Short Architectural History of Worcester Cathedral.
Worcester: Philip Barker

Grundy, M (ed), 1997 Worcester at Work: Portrait of a Victorian City.
Worcester : Osborne Books

Hughes, P, 2002 Saving Worcester from the Bulldozer.
Worcester: Mayor's lecture

Knowles, J M, 1995 College Green Worcester 1800-1900. Worcester:
Worcester Cathedral

McMenemy W H, 1947 *History of the Worcester Royal Infirmary.*
London: Press Alliances

Morriss R K, 1994 *The Buildings of Worcester.*
Stroud: Alan Sutton Publishing

Pevsner N, *The Buildings of England: Worcestershire.* London: Penguin

Simpkin P, 1996 *Red Hill School Worcester, 1896-1996.*
Malvern: Images Publishing

## Schooling

Browne E O (ed), 1933 *Fifty Years of the Alice Ottley School, Worcester.*
Worcester: Caxton Press

Craze M, 1972 *King's School, Worcester 1541-1971.* Worcester: Ebenezer
Baylis The Trinity Press

Doolan B, 1996  *St. George's Catholic Church Worcester: a Brief Guide.*
Worcester: St. George's Catholic Church

Griffith G, 1870 Going to Markets and Grammar Schools, vol. 2.
London: W Freeman

Gwilliam B, 1993 *Old Worcester: People and Places.*
Bromsgrove: Halfshire Press (I am greatly indebted to this book for
information on Education in Worcester)

Hounds Lane Board School, 1887 *Admission register*

Knowles J M, 1999 Huntingdon Hall: *Chapel to Concert Hall, the Countess
of Huntington and her Chapel at Worcester.* Worcester: Huntingdon Friends

Sandon H, 1978 *Worcester Royal Porcelain from 1862 to the Present. 3rd ed.*
London: Barrie and Jenkins

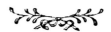

## Transport

Abbott E & Glover, C, 1967 *A History of Worcester City Police 1833-1967* Worcester: Worcester.City Council

Cobbett W, 1948 *Rural Rides*, v. 2 London: Dent (Everyman's Library)

Demaus, A B, 1973 *Fifty Years of the Bicycle in Worcestershire 1880-1930.* Worcester: City Walls Press

Grundy M (ed), 1997 *Worcester at Work: Portrait of a Victorian City.* Worcester: Osborne Books

Hanson H, 1984 *The Canal Boatmen 1760-1914.* Gloucester: Alan Sutton

Ordnance Survey, 1996 *Old Ordnance Survey Maps: Worcester sheet N.E.* Alan Godfrey Maps. Facsimile reprint of map published by the Ordnance Survey, 1902 Introductory essay by John Boynton

Storer P, The Nineteenth Century Railway in Worcester. Manchester: Unpublished University of Manchester BA assignment

Winspear, S, 1996 *Worcester's Lost Theatre.* Parkbarn Press

## Politics

Abbott E & Glover, C, 1967 *A History of Worcester City Police, 1833-1967.* Worcester: Worcester City Council

Barnsby G J, 1977 *The Working Class Movement in the Black Country.* Wolverhampton: Integrated Publishing Series

*Berrows Journal* 24 February 1842 See for extract on the lively public meeting in the Guildhall

Carpenter J H, 1972/3 *The Amalgamated Society of Engineers: the Study of a Victorian Trades Union, Worcester branch.* Worcester: Amalgamated Society of Engineers

Craze M, 1972 *King's School Worcester*, 1541-1971. Worcester: Ebenezer Baylis

Creighton L, 1904 *Life and Letters of Mandell Creighton*, v. 1. London: Longmans Green

Gaut R C, 1939 *A History of Worcestershire Agriculture.* Worcester: Littlebury

Gwilliam, B, 1993 Old Worcester: People and Places. Bromsgrove, Halfshire Books (I am grateful for these and other insights from Bill Gwilliam's books)

Hadfield A M, 1970 The Chartist Land Company. Newton Abbot: David & Charles

Royal Commission into Election Bribery in Worcester, 1906 *Judge's Report (with evidence)* London: HMSO

Turberville T C, 1852 *Worcestershire in the Nineteenth Century.* London: Longmans

**For all later Victorian parliamentary elections see:**
Williams W R, 1897 The Parliamentary History of the County of Worcester Hereford: W R Williams

**Religion**

Barker P, 1994 *A Short Architectural history of Worcester Cathedral.* Worcester: Worcester Cathedral Publications

Boast A H, *A Complete History of Angel Street Congregational Church Worcester 1687-1965.* Worcester:Published by Angel Street Congregational Church

Bridges T, 2000 *Churches of Worcestershire. Logaston,* Herefordshire: Logaston Press

Carpenter J H, 1972/3 *The Amalgamated Society of Engineers: the Study of a Victorian Trades Union, Worcester branch.* Worcester: Amalgamated Society of Engineers

Gwilliam B, 1993 *Old Worcester: People and Places.* Bromsgrove: Halfshire

Hughes P A, 1984 *A Cloud of Witnesses: A History of Bromyard Road Methodist Church.* Worcester: Bromyard Road Methodist Church

Kelway C, 1933, *The Story of the Catholic Revival, 1833-1933, 4th ed.* London: Phillip Allan

Kilvert F, 1960 *Diary of Francis Kilvert.* Edited by W Plomer. London: J Cape

Knowles J M, 1999 *Huntingdon Hall: Chapel to Concert Hall, the Countess of Huntington and her Chapel at Worcester.* Worcester: Huntingdon Friends (I am grateful to this author for all the references to the Countess of Huntingdon's Chapel)

136

Lockett, R, 1978 George Gilbert Scott, the Joint Restoration Committee and the Refurnishing of Worcester Cathedral 1863-1874. *Worcestershire Archaeological Society Transactions*, Third Series, 6

## Victorian Specialities

### Worcestershire Sauce

Keogh B, 1997 *The Secret Sauce: a History of Lea and Perrins.* Worcester: Leaper Books
*I am indebted to this most informative book for the information in this chapter.*

### Porcelain

Jones R, 1993 Porcelain in Worcester 1751-1951: *an Illustrated Social History*. Hallow: Parkbarn

Sandon H, *Royal Worcester Porcelain from 1862 to the Present Day.* Barrie and Jenkins

Sandon J, 1993 *The Dictionary of Worcester Porcelain 1751-1851.* Woodbridge, Suffolk: Antique Collectors' Club. 2 v.

### Worcester Shopping

Bridges T and Mundy, C, 1996 *Worcester: a Pictorial History.* Chichester: Phillimore

Gaut R C, 1939 *A History of Worcester Agriculture.* Worcester: Littlebury

Gwilliam B, *Old Worcester: People and Places.* Bromsgrove: Halfshire

Haynes C and M, 1986 *Old Worcester as Seen through the Camera.* Buckingham: Barracuda Books

Hibbert C, 1987 *The English: a Social History, 1066-1945.* London: Grafton Books

*Littlebury's Directory for 1868.* Worcester: Littlebury Press

Mathias P, 1967 *Retailing Revolution.* London: Longmans

Roberts R, 1990 *The Classic Slum: Salford life in the First Quarter of the Century.* London: Penguin

### Elgar, the Victorian

Grundy M, *Elgar Birthplace Guide.* The Elgar Foundation

Grundy M, 1984 *Elgar's Beloved Country*.
Worcester: Worcester City Council

Leicester H, 1930 *Forgotten Worcester*. Worcester: E. Baylis
Introduction by Sir Edward Elgar

## Benjamin Leader Williams

Dean D, *Benjamin Williams Leader*: Victorian Painter. Worcester:
Worcester City Council

Lusk L, 1901 *The Art annual* 1901

## Busier Days at the Guildhall

*City of Worcester Year Books*, 1880-1899. Worcester: Worcester City
Council, printed by Deighton and Co.

## Naturalists

Jones M M, 1947 *The Lookers Out of Worcestershire*. The Worcestershire
Naturalists Club

Symonds W S, 1999 *Hanley Castle - An Episode of the Civil wars and the
Battle of Worcester*. Great Malvern: Cappella Archive

## The Battle of the Stained Glass

Barnes, G, 1984 *Frederick Preedy: Architect and Glass Painter, 1820-1898*.
Stroud: Alan Sutton Publications

Binnall P B G, 1973-74 The Adelaide Memorial Window in Worcester
Cathedral. *Journal of the British Society of Master Glass-Painters*, 15 (2)

## Exotic and Novel Interludes at the Museum

Jones M M, 1947 *The Lookers Out of Worcestershire*. The Worcestershire
Naturalists Club

# Index

140

Cartwright, General, HM Inspector Constabulary 82
cast iron 17
castle site 1
Cathedral school 119
Catholic church in Sansome Place See St George Roman Catholic Church
Catholic school 62
cattle market 4
celebrities' receptions 8
cemetery, municipal 54
Census of Religious Worship, 1851 27
Chamberlain, Jo 85
Chamberlain and Co. 28, 101
Chang the Chinese Giant 8
chapels 54
charities 3, 39
Chartist Land Plan 40, 78
Chartist activity in Worcester 32, 78
Chartists: imprisoned in Worcester 32
Cheltenham 11
Cheltenham Race Course 44
chemists 98
Chief of Police 27
cholera 30, 36, 116
Christian, Ewart 51
churches: All Saints (52), Angel Street Congregational Chapel (52), Baptist Chapel (94, 96),
Barbourne Wesleyan (28), Congregational Chapel in Angel Place (61), Countess of
Huntingdon Sunday School (61), Episcopalian Floating Chapel (27), Holy Trinity Church (93),
Lady Huntingdon's Connection: congregation and chapel (96), Pump Street Wesleyan (28),
Quaker meeting house (94), St Barnabas (93), St Clement's (52), St George Roman Catholic
Church (53, 93, 109), St George's Barbourne (52), St Johns Wesleyan (28), St Martins in the
Cornmarket (2), St Mary's in the Arboretum (52), St Nicholas (52), St Pauls (31), St Pauls in
the Blockhouse (93), St Stephen's Barbourne (52), Stretton Grandison Parish Church (125),
Zion Chapel (95)
churches, new 52
churches, restoration 52
cider 23
cigarettes 104
circus 8
City and County Bank 55
City and County Laundry 50
city boundaries 1
City Council Manure 117
City of Worcester Ship 69
City Steam Confectionary Works 21
Clark, George, government public health inspector 27, 30
clergy 89
Clifton, Henry 77
clog and patten makers 5
clothing and drapery stores 106
clothing firms 5
coaches 24, 70
coaching inns 24
Cobbett, William 68
coffee lounges 29
College Green 52, 89
College of the Blind: music 110
Commandery building 66
commercial buildings 55-56
concentration of poor inhabitants in the city centre 30
Congregational Chapel in Angel Place 61
Congregationalist Chapel 94
conservatism, its effectiveness in political organization 83
Conservatives and Unionists 82
Coomber, F W 73

fox hunting 44
friendly societies 38
        Buffaloes (38), Oddfellows (38), Recabites (38)
        fruit wines 19, 29
fruits and vegetables, varieties of 5
funfair operators 7
game law trial 75
garden furniture 17
Gardeners Arms 24
Garibaldi, Giuseppe 8, 25,
gas supply 116
Gas Works (Rainbow Hill) 55
General Market 53
gentleman's apparel 16, 107
gentry and trade 48
Gilbert & Sullivan 12
gin drinking 27
gin shops 27
girls' school 66
glee clubs 13
Gloucester (Marquis of Granby) 25
glove liners 17
Glover, Maria (grocery shop) 104
Glover Street, now New Street 16, 16
gloveresses 17
gloves, special 17
gloving industry 16-17, 35
        Dents (16), Fownes (16)
The Golden Lion 25, 26
Gomershal, William, actor manager 12, 83
government financial aid 61
Government School of Design 67, 102, 112
Grainger's 101, 103
Grand National Consolidated Trades Union, Worcester branch 40
Grand Templar Malins  See Malins, Joseph
Great Western Railway 73
Great Western Railway (suppliers of clocks, watches, and chronometers to the railway) 20
Great Witley 42, 45, 46
Green Dragon, Bewdley 25
Green Man Inn 24
'green stuff' market 4
Greening, Ann 26
Gregory's Bank Brick Works 55
Griffiths, George 42, 64
groceries 104
groceries: prices 104
Grossmith, B 127
Guesten Hall 93, 121
Guildhall 26, 80, 114-119
Guildhall finances 114
Guildhall meetings 77
Guildhall: public meeting in 1842 79
Guildhall restoration 51
gymnastics 10
Hadley, James 67, 101, 102, 103
Hagley Hall 46
Hall of Science 95
hangings 33
Hangman Berry 26
Hanson, J S 61
Hardy and Padmore 17
Hartlebury Castle 41, 52
Hastings, Charles 80, 32, 120
Hastings, Charles: contribution to public health in Worcester 36

147

148

152

# Acknowledgements

Two leading British historians, Edward and Dorothy Thompson, who lived in this area were a true inspiration but I also owe much to the work of skilful popularisers like Bill Gwilliam and Mike Grundy as well as a new generation of talented local historians. To the Worcester Porcelain Museum and The City of Worcester Museum Service amongst others, I am extremely grateful for permission to use illustrative material and I also owe a special debt to Charity Mitchell, Jane Thorniley - Walker, Barbara Ronchetti, Mark Hogan and Stuart Burton for their efforts in preparing the text. Every endeavour has been made to contact any owners of copyright.

This writing project has kept me out of trouble for several years for I wished to write something, however inadequate, in memory of my mother and father and my sister and brother-in-law. If any royalties are earned, they will go to one of Worcester's local charities and the hope of a better world.

Jeff Carpenter  March 2006

# Jeff Carpenter

*Jeff's local history courses at 'Worcester Tech.' were widely enjoyed and he was amongst those who started up the Victorian Fair as well as Worcester's Green Badge Tourists guides. Jeff has produced a number of books on local history and these days contributes a regular heritage column in the Worcestershire Now magazine. As a former West Midland Heritage Lottery Committee Chairman, he has always been keen to see substantial lottery funds invested back into the county.*

*Jeff Carpenter was once Mayor of Worcester and under the terms of an ancient local charity could now be claiming consideration as 'a decayed councillor or alderman of the City of Worcester'. 'You never know when that could come in handy', he says.*

*'Jeff Carpenter has done a cracking job with his latest book* Victorian Worcester - *a biography'*

Mike Pryce - *Worcester Evening News*